From Gramsci to Freud:

7 Anti-Christian Philosophers Who Ruined America

Dr. Michael J. Baglino, Ed. D.

ALL RIGHTS RESERVED
COPYRIGHT © 2023
BY MICHAEL J. BAGLINO
Printed in the United States of America
First Printing Edition, 2023

ISBN: 979-8-8692-6035-2

All Biblical Quotes are from

The Holy Bible, ESV. 2001. Wheaton, IL.: Crossway.

New American Bible. 2011. Washington, D. C. : World Catholic Press.

Dedication

– I wonder if the faculty of Winona State University [WSU] in Minnesota and Florida International University [FIU] in Miami teaches the premise of this book to its students today. I know that the 60s [Winona State] and the 80s [FIU] gave me the background needed to write this. Along with some personal experiences of living around the U. S. A. and visiting Europe often, I learned perspectives on these matters that built up over the years. I give special thanks to Dr. Daniel Hoyt and Dr. James Eddy of Winona State and Dr. Carlos Alvarez, Dr. Steve Fain and Dr. Miguel Escotet of FIU who were surely influential intellectually on these matters. I in no way consider myself an intellectual. I just continued with wanting to know about this world, admittedly and probably Eurocentrically. Read a lot and expanded my views globally at FIU. My mind was always filled with social philosophy to help explain things to myself. What was going on? Still not original, I also owe much to Pastor Adrian Rogers, Christian radio and TV preacher from whom I heard a great sermon and lecture on the radio : *5 Anti*

Christian Philosophers Who Ruined America. Here are seven with some extras.

Introduction One

This is the fourth book for me, a fifth on its way this summer. Raised Catholic and very Italian in Brooklyn and Long Island New York, ours was a rather traditional family. In the 1950s Nassau County in Long island was a conservative stronghold. Combine that with a Department of Defense civilian official as a father, with an entrepreneurial side to him, conservative politics was the perspective. Then again, combine that with being loyal New York Yankee fans, the epitome of corporate America, it only seemed logical my father and mother registered Republican. I did too in my mind. I began working for the department of defense myself, and my world view was set.

Winona State College [our humble institution, now university] was where I attended college. This is located in a conservative river town in southern Minnesota, bible belt America. In Winona, Christianity was everywhere and the middle American Anglo culture surely dominated. My first political science professor was angry at his home country, the Philippines, for choosing not to become a new American state when it had its opportunity to do so. He also liked my essays on the conservative economic policies of President Kennedy. This was 1962. Pro America all the way.

Then something happened - the 60s. I guess I was a privileged American kid as my folks paid for most of my college. Consequently, I became one of those identifying with the college radicals throughout the country and their celebrity. I learned Marxism mostly through author Erich Fromm, socialist, social philosopher and neo-Freudian psychoanalyst. Plus, I wasn't going to church. There you have it, a college lefty. I attribute these days as a time for learning about the left and not really becoming a true follower. How do I know this? When you go back to church and consciously commit to Christ, rather than being the less than mindful cradle Catholic I was, all false ideologies fall by the wayside.

So, with an understanding of the Marxist and liberal mindset and a background in conservatism, adulthood became a journey of what people might refer to as open mindedness finally settling in with my Catholic Christian world view. And that is what it is, Catholic, neither left nor right, no matter what others accuse. And that is either, politically, socially or psychologically.

But I remember it to this day, nearly 60 years later. What was the most influential college experience, though many, to which I can attribute my understanding of the left / right continuum of thought in politics. It was Dr. James Eddy's graduate class, American Foreign Policy. Some of the senior citizens reading this introduction can appreciate this. Pretty much a seminar class, though Dr. Eddy spoke the most, we had the responsibility of reading three books with class discussion. One from the left, one from the right and one from the center. Those books were Erich Fromm, *May Man Prevail*; Robert Strausz Hupe, *Protracted Conflict*; Henry Kissinger, *Necessity for Choice*.

Erich Fromm in *May Man Prevail,* maintained that as the Soviet society grew economically with a rising middle class, it would soften its belligerence against the west. He called for mutual disarmament. This was the leftist view. Robert Strauz Hupe in *Protracted Conflict* maintained along with much factual research, the deviousness, dishonesty and deceit of the Soviets and their strategy. He identified the Soviet system an immoral one in foundation and in practice and called for a protracted conflict against them as they had against us. This was the right wing view. Henry Kissinger's book *Necessity for Choice*, was an outline of necessary strategies on many fronts throughout the cold war. It was non ideological and a practical approach to our pressing dilemma with communism. This was considered the moderate view at the time. You might call these works outdated but their ideas and approaches live on. In fact, I just might cite these three authors here in the *7 Anti-Christian Philosophers Who Ruined America*. You can also call this book a primer on America's current communist revolution. So many believe it cannot happen here. It is happening, 21st century style.

From Gramsci to Freud:
7 Anti-Christian Philosophers

Who Ruined America, and How the Left Follows Their Philosophies

Contents

Dedication i
Introduction One... iii
Introduction Two - The Seven Philosophers 1
   Chapter 1: 7 Anti-Christian Philosophers Who Ruined America..2
   Chapter 2: Left vs. Right on the Political Spectrum 13
   Chapter 3: The Democrat Party from a Catholic's Perspective.. 20

Part I: Philosopher 1 - Antonio Gramsci................................ 26
   Chapter 4: Gramsci and the Left Today 27
   Chapter 5: The Attack on Columbus: Gramsci All the Way 38
   Chapter 6: Social Disorganization as a Way to a Centralized State 43

Part II: Philosopher 2 - Herbert Marcuse............................... 51
   Chapter 7: Herbert Marcuse and the Left Today.................52
   Chapter 8: Professional Revolutionaries in the U. S. 57
   Chapter 9: Critical Race Theory and the Marxist Putcsh... 64

PART III: Philosopher 3 - Georg Hegel 70
   Chapter 10: Georg Hegel and the Left Today......................71
   Chapter 11: Are So Called Liberals Today Really Liberal? ..77

Part IV Philosopher 4 - Ludwig Feuerbach 83
   Chapter 12: Feuerbach and the Left Today 84
   Chapter 13: What Might Marxist University Professors be Responsible For? - An Eyewitness Account 91

Part V: Philosopher 5 - Karl Marx 97
   Chapter 14: Just What is Marxism Anyway? 98
   Chapter 15: What Factors Contribute to Economic Development? 108
   Chapter 16: Marx's Communism via Marcuse: New Millennium Style 115

Part VI: Philosopher 6 - Charles Darwin 123
   Chapter 17: Charles Darwin and the Left Today 124
   Chapter 18: Freedom, Determinism and Authority 131

Part VII: Philosopher 7 - Sigmund Freud 137
   Chapter 19: Sigmund Freud and the Left Today 138
   Chapter 20: Neuroticism in America 146
   Chapter 21: Psychological Narcissism and the Administrative State 157

PART VIII: Christianity and Socialism 165
   Chapter 22: Socialism from a Catholic's Perspective 166
   Chapter 23: Only Mass Enrollment in Christian Schools Can Save this Country 175
   Chapter 24: 4 Characteristics Needed for Christian Leadership: The Future 182
   Chapter 25: What is Servant Leadership? 185
   Chapter 26 The Ongoing Prejudices: Anti-Catholicism and Anti Semitism 191
   Chapter 27: SUMMARY and CONCLUSION 201
References: 207

Introduction Two - The Seven Philosophers

Chapter 1:

7 Anti-Christian Philosophers Who Ruined America

They tell us this all the time. We are out of the mainstream. We have become extremist. The liberal establishment is intent on painting those outside of their ideological mindset as extremist and threats to our democracy. All hogwash; it is them. The anticommunist Democrat Party is no way similar to its 1960s past as it embraces leftist ideology. It's like the psychopath who denies others' definitions of himself as a psychopath until his behaviors are too much for him to deny. It all catches up with him. It'll all catch up to the Democrats. It's caught up.

Where did it begin? Aside from the urban residence of most Democrats where media and lifestyle have such an enormous effect on the population, the Democrat Party itself is led by an intelligentsia immersed in European secular philosophy. Though this humble writer outlined much on this topic in his article "5 Anti-Christian

Philosophers Who Ruined America" [Baglino, 2022], I will add the focus on two other philosophers who more recently influence western thought taken on by Democrat leaders: the more contemporary Antonio Gramsci and Herbert Marcuse.

Antonio Gramsci

Antonio Gramsci is probably the most influential European social and economic theorist of the 20th century. He is referred to as a neo-Marxist by proclaiming his opposition to capitalism and supporting public ownership of wealth and property. Since capitalist societies are controlled by ideology and cultural means, Gramsci called for the systematic attack on its ideology and breakdown of its culture. This included an attack on Christianity which Gramsci believed the glue of the culture. Only this could alter the people's consciousness and thus pave the way toward a progressive civil society.

He referred to his theory as 'cultural hegemony' advocating the working class join forces with minorities in order to bring on revolutionary change and bring down the capitalist ruling class. The intelligentsia would have the responsibility to promote the change.

Herbert Marcuse

Historians give Herbert Marcuse most of the credit for inspiring student uprisings and rebellions of the 1960s in both Europe and the United States. Referred to as 'the guru of the new left', and proud of his notoriety, Marcuse maintained that both continents, especially the United States were actually repressive societies - politically, economically, humanistically and sexually, and called for freedom seeking youth to rebel against it. This included criticism of the foundation of its culture, Christianity. He inspired media famous revolutionaries such as Abbie Hoffman, Rudy Deutschke, Angela Davis, and Daniel Cohn-Bendit. His works such as *One-Dimensional Man* and *Eros and Civilization* were on top of the reading list for America's *Students for a Democratic Society [SDS]* and Italy's *Le Brigate Rosse*. Democrat Party leaders today are students of the 60s. Marcuse was their intellectual hero. President Biden is no intellectual, but rather a lifelong career bureaucrat and follower of the pack;

no leader is he. I'm sure he doesn't know who Marcuse is.

Radio and TV evangelist Adrian Rogers once gave a short radio presentation entitled *5 Philosophers that Ruined America*. Could be a good college lecture. I thought I would elaborate a bit on that topic to help explain the current downward trajectory of our country, culture and western civilization in general. Thus the above cited article based on that lecture. These additional not so contemporary 5 philosophers are Georg Hegel, Karl Marx, Ludwig Feuerbach, Charles Darwin and Sigmund Freud.

Georg Hegel

Georg Hegel [pronounced geh-org hey-gul] was a 17th and 18th century German philosopher who was militantly atheistic and anti-Christian. A precursor to Karl Marx, he promoted concepts that he hoped would ultimately lead to national and world dictatorship. Based on the sociological concepts of phenomenology and cultural relativity, the idea was to create conflict within the culture in order to bring about government control as its remedy - one of those being a specific opposition to Christian religious values. State intervention would be necessary to resolve differences of religion, social mores, race, peace and war, ideologies, political groups, economic interests of workers and business owners. Conflict theory and critical race theory as taught in western university social and behavioral science classes have George Hegel's dialectic as its foundation.

Ludwig Feuerbach

Ludwig Feuerbach was yet another German atheistic philosopher extremely critical of Christianity. He maintained we didn't need religion any longer and could develop humanistic and rational philosophies without it. With atheism Feurerbach believed we can help man reach his potential because our lives were developed as much as could be given the economic circumstances. Thus, we don't really need God and the 'God is Dead' movement began. Technological control would surely lead us out of our dependence of a man-made creation, religion and Christianity. An industrial revolution visionary.

Karl Marx

Karl Marx restructured this dialectic referred to as a conflict of thesis and anti-thesis eventually leading through historical struggle to a synthesis of knowledge and perception. He focused on economic conflict between workers and owners of the means of production called dialectic materialism. Marx believed all of world history was a history of material want and class struggle between these groups. God and religion were in its way. He despised religion, especially Judaism and the Lutheran Church. The 'opiate of the people' was his mantra about religion.

The father of communism is a title often attributed to Karl Marx. Das Kapital and The Communist Manifesto are among his most famous works. The socialist and communist revolution of the working class against the bourgeoisie [management and middle class] was the only way to cure the ills of a capitalist society, and religion supported capitalism. Both must go. These ideas were instrumental in bringing about the communist countries of The Soviet Union, Peoples Republic of China, Cuba, North Korea and Khmer Rouge dictatorship in

Cambodia. All were responsible for the killing of millions.

Charles Darwin

Charles Darwin was Christian and had intentions of becoming an Anglican minister. His education at the University of Edinburgh and Cambridge influence him to take another direction as a geologist and biologist. Darwin's famous *Theory of Biological Evolution* stated that all species of organisms arise and develop through the natural selection of small, inherited variations that increase the individual's ability to compete, survive, and reproduce. However, he believed his evolutionary theory could be reconciled through Christianity as sort of synthesis. Maybe change Christianity to conform to his theory. Similarly suggested recently by Hillary Clinton: Christianity must conform to the times and our way of thinking. This too resembles the Catholic church's conflict with the secular notion *liberation theology*, a neo-Marxist construct. Darwinian theory of evolution is in direct opposition to creationist theory of various Christian religions found within Protestantism. The theory of Evolution relegates humans as similar and even equal to the animal kingdom in most aspects of biology. Does the name PETA ring a bell? It is competition and survival of the fittest that motivates humans. In that same vein, and unlike Christianity and modern feminism, Darwin had a dim view of women as not equal to men in that evolution.

The principles established in Social Darwinism, a sociological construct, justify acts of racism and thoughts of ethnic superiority. Proponents argue certain human races and ethnic groups have desirable and strong traits. These groups dominate perceived weaker and flawed groups, and deserve dominion. In Europe, German leader Adolph Hitler used the theory of Social Darwinism to declare the Aryan race supreme and others, particularly Jews and other minorities, inferior.

Herbert Spencer, a 19th-century philosopher, receives credit for conceiving the theory of Social Darwinism. So Spencer becomes and integral part of Darwinian theory. Spencer considered the government in Europe established by white's superior in technology, economy and structure to governments elsewhere in the world. Spencer stated natural selection played out in the military and economic dominance of European countries led by white rulers. The strong white race gained power while "inferior" races lagged behind. It justified colonialism and imperialism at the time, suggesting Asian, Black and Indigenous populations were not as capable as their European colonizers.

Sigmund Freud

Finally, we arrive at the infamous Sigmund Freud, an atheistic, anti- Christian philosopher, Jewish in name only. Our 7th philosopher, Freud not only hated Catholicism and Christianity in general, he was extremely fearful of Rome itself, refusing to visit there. The spectre of Catholicism in Rome haunted him as a threat to his authoritarian mindset and beliefs. He hated when people disagreed with him. A native of Austria, Freud disavowed any spirituality and focused on the physical aspects, especially sexual motivations, the mind, biology and behavior. Called the father of modern psychology, he coined phrases such as id and ego, conscious and subconscious, reality principle, and various defense mechanisms supporting sexual motivations. Essentially man was motivated by biological impulses of sex and aggression and any spirituality assigned to humans were limiting of freedom. Only by unleashing rather than repressing sexuality, as he believed religion did, could man realize his true self. He had to be released from the constraints of family and society which was too burdened by a Christian culture. The anti-Christian values of the free sex movement of the 60s and Gay marriage initiatives, though Freud was against homosexuality as a sort of arrested development, are attributed to the Freudian philosophy.

Conflicts within the ideas of these philosophies and with the social organization of western culture once dominated by Christianity are playing out to this day. Marxism, conflict theory, critical race theory, technological control, governmental and corporate totalitarian control, breakdown and change in sexual mores on a national and even global scale are the issues of the modern era. We can trace them to the above seven philosophers.

Sources:

Baglino, Michael J. 2022. "5 Anti-Christian Philosophers Who Ruined America. www.Catholic365.com

Fromm, Erich. 1962. *Beyond the Chains of Illusion: My Encounter with Marx and Freud.* New York: Bloomsbury.

Krason, Stephen A. 2022. "What the Democratic Party has Become." *The Catholic Social Science Review.* Vol. 27. The Society of Catholic Social Scientists.

Rogers, Adrian. "Five Anti-Christian Philosophers Who Ruined America. Palm City, FL: WCNO Radio.

Chapter 2:

Left vs. Right on the Political Spectrum

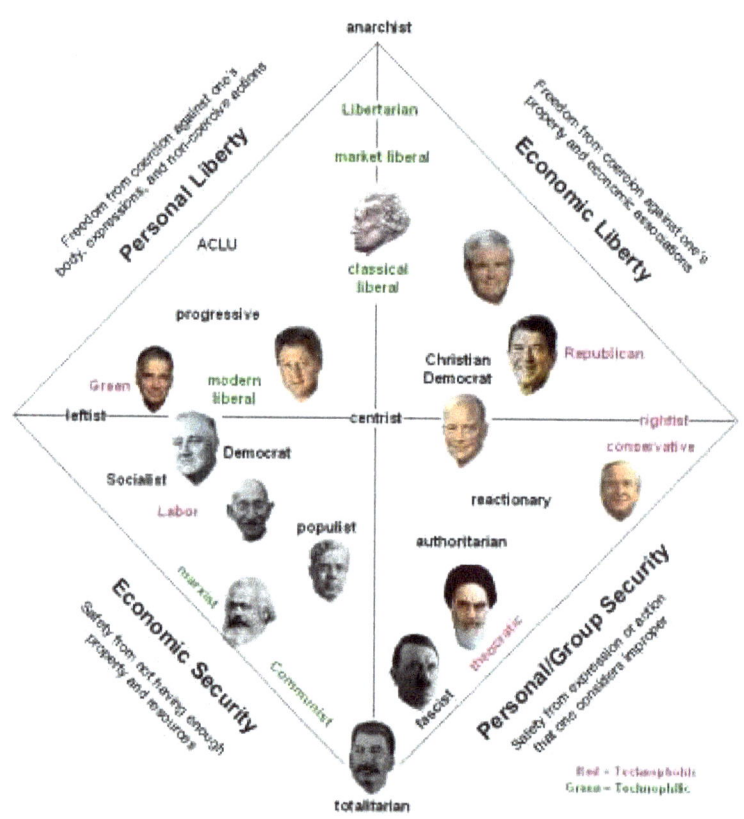

Pinterest

Sometimes political scientists draw a line from left to right to help explain political philosophies.

Sometimes they draw a circle. The diagram above is I believe fairly clear in that if we start on the central vertical line, we see on the right the term **rightist**. Traditionally the right wing as been supportive of inequality. By this we refer to maintaining a social system of inequality as the proper way of things. That is, inequality of classes, inequality of incomes, of races, of gender, of religions, of occupations; etc. Governments exist to maintain that inequality so as to keep the proper order. Thus, the former governments of South Africa, Germany, Spain for example maintained a society separating races, or religions, or ethnic groups as the natural order based on history. We call that fascism or Nazism. Hitler/Germany and Franco/Spain were referred to as right wing Fascists. The term *totalitarian* regimes apply since such nations require *total* control of all institutions in society and the lives of the people who participate in them - educational, political, religious, economic, family, health institutions. We will return to the term *totalitarian* at the end of this article.

As we proceed to the left, the extreme right is modified and represents a more authoritarian society, not so much under total control, but with the intent on law and order first, religious dominance second. Islamic nations and military dictatorships like Iran or some Central American countries fall into this category. These governments are usually at the behest and dominance of the wealthy classes in keeping political control. Or as the case in Iran, a religious hegemony.

The center of the spectrum lists varying types of democracies supporting both individual and economic freedoms. Personal and economic liberties refer to freedom of speech, religion, press, assembly, association, and free market capitalism, all supported by and with the graces of the government, state or federal. Some democracies limit their size of government to allow more freedom, while some believe government is needed to protect these freedoms. Democracies try to maintain a government run of, by and for the people without any one person or group having too much power, especially centralized power. The greatest threat to freedom in democracies would be large scale organizations controlling the society such as corporations or governments. The United States and many European nations have always been the exemplary representatives of democracy; however, such nations today have grown their central governments to the point of more centralized control. Where are we going now?

Here's where - to the left. Here is where governments increase again in size, control and power, all for the good of society as they say. Government exists to help the poor, the homeless, the disenfranchised, those on the margins, the oppressed minorities held back from their own progress. It is the growth of government bureaucracy seeking to expand its purposes. Large scale governments are watchdogs over corporate misbehaviors such as environmental pollution, pharmaceutical abuses or worker exploitation. They help instill the social conscience of the corporate world, All are worthy responsibilities for sure in today's complicated world. How many more babies would be deformed if Thalidomide was not banned or how many more lakes and rivers would be polluted if corporate waste were not restricted? Today large scale centralized governments expand power to protect abortion rights or fight climate change. Many will say large scale centralized governmental bureaucracies have now gone too far.

It all leads us to the far left of the spectrum. The ideologies of socialism and communism are at the far left. Government control and even dictatorship is believed necessary to control a society based on equality as opposed to fascist inequality. It is a governmental system forcing an equality of incomes, occupational levels, status, and material being. They call this equity. The state is considered the higher power and it becomes jealous of any competing powers such as the extreme wealthy or religious groups. It is run by an elitist group and becomes totalitarian in that it must impose and maintain a society of equality and equity among all social institutions - education, political, religious, economic, family, health. This is not unlike the totalitarian dictatorships on the right mentioned above. China, the former Soviet Union, North Korea, Vietnam, Cuba, and Cambodia under the Khmer Rouge are representatives of the socialist and communist ideologies.

And guess what, they hate the fascists on the right. Their intent is to grow their governments and instill change in all democracies through nefarious means of deceit, dishonesty and deviousness. The ends justifies the means. Then by taking control their Marxist [communist] utopia can now begin. They take control by forcing all other ideologies to take sides between them and the growing fascist resistance. As the left in their revolutionary quest pushes its enemies away from them, the resisting group coagulates into one and labeled fascists. Anyone more conservative than them is call fascist. How is this done? Well, let me refer you to an article this author wrote, "5 Philosophers Who Ruined America" listed under sources below.

Anarchy and revolution is the desired result; it's the final confrontation between left and right. Chaos, disorganization, violence between racial and ethnic groups, neighborhoods, workers and management, with communism as the sought after outcome. Today the word is 'progressive' not 'communist' and so the 'new world order' begins. [See, "Just What is Marxism Anyway?" in this book]. So which side are you on: right, middle, center? Which will you fight for?

Sources:

Baglino, Michael J. 2022. *5 Anti-Christian Philosophers Who Ruined America.* Catholic365.com

Baglino, Michael J. 2023. *Florida Meets Europe.* NY: LT Publishing.

Chapter 3:

The Democrat Party from a Catholic's Perspective

We all know this. We can all write this. But Stephen A. Krason [2022] published this, so let me summarize and yet insert some of my own experiences and insights.

They tell us this all the time. We are out of the mainstream. We have become extremist. The liberal establishment is intent on painting those outside of their ideological mindset as extremist and threats to our democracy. All hogwash; it is them.

Historians give Herbert Marcuse most of the credit for inspiring student uprisings and rebellions of the 1960s in both Europe and the United States. I repeat from Ch. 1, Marcuse is referred to as 'the guru of the new left'. He maintained that both continents, especially the United States were actually repressive societies - politically, economically, humanistically and sexually, and called for freedom seeking youth to rebel against it. This included criticism of the foundation of its culture, Christianity. He inspired media famous revolutionaries such as Abbie Hoffman, Rudy Duetschke, Angela Davis, and Daniel Cohn-Bendit. His works such as *One Dimensional Man* and *Eros and Civilization* were on top of the reading list for America's *Students for a Democratic Society [SDS]* and *Italy's Le Brigatte Rosse*.

The Democrat Party of today is not the antcommunist Democrat Party of the 1960s. The Republican Party of today **is** the Republican Party of the 1960s. Democrat President Kennedy's policies, 1961 - 1963, mirrors Republican policy today. The new left focused its rebellions against the Democrat Party in the 1960s as the perpetrators of the Vietnam war. According to Professor Stephen M. Krason, the Democrat party "has become the party of irrationality, fantasy, hypocrisy, disregarding the rule of law for reasons of political opportunism, and repression of those who dare not share its ideological preferences."

By irrationality he means embracing transgenderism, that open borders have no effect on crime or national security or disease. Being a party of fantasy refers the claim of systematic racism as never defined and that equal opportunity laws are greater than ever. By hypocrisy is its complicity to the riots of 2020 which Antifa and BLM organized and promulgated. Further hypocrisy is when they disregard rule of law and support illegal immigration. Also it is when they refuse to enforce the law as demonstrators harass Supreme Court justices at their homes. Democrat opportunism is the allowing illegal immigration with the belief that the newly arrived will be a voting block for them. Repression by Democrats is the harassment of storming the homes President Trump or pro-life activists. It is pressuring cable companies to not allow conservative news networks. It is calling parents terrorists for opposing the BLM and Critical Race Theory Marxist curriculums in the public schools.

How do you confront and turn the tide on this growing repression which takes its orders from its Marxist philosophical base? Professor Krason calls for letter writing and phone calling campaigns to governors, legislators, university administrators and corporate executives. Further, he asks us to reach out to alumni and hold back donations to their graduating institutions. Finally we would need religious organizations and religious groups to partner and work out a battle plan. This humble author calls for parents to remove their children from the public schools and universities and send them to Catholic and other private Christian schools.

Finally, Professor Krason [2022] talks about racism which to the Democrats is only anti Black racism. Prejudice is of course a sin for which all are guilty in varying degrees. Only one person on this planet had no prejudice and He was crucified for it. Sociologists over and over again point out the breakdown of the Black family which is at the root of many of their problems. Fatherless homes, lack of role models, lack of church attendance by males, poor community leadership as we witness the Al Sharptons and Jesse Jacksons of the world. Never once have I heard these two gentlemen proclaim and evangelize the name of Jesus, Him and Him crucified as Christians are called to do; nor do their behaviors reflect any gifts of the Holy Spirit.

The recent defection of presidential candidate Tulsi Gabbard from the Democrat Party further highlights their extremism. Herself a woman of faith, she condemned the Democrats as woke and cowardly who are hostile to people of faith. She maintains that they racialize every issue and even flatter the idea of anti white racism as acceptable. Further she sees them demonizing the police and favoring criminals over law abiding citizens. The Democrats in turn accused Ms. Gabbard as a favorite of the Russians; it's always the Russians. And as an army military officer, she feels she can no longer be a part of their ideological adherence to the Marxist agendas thus calling independent thinkers to join her.

No, the Democrat Party is an irresponsible lot, seeking power of government control rather than focusing on root causes of problems. Root causes, you hear them mention that phrase often. Well, here are the root causes: lack of God and breakdown of family. Any society without God and family is destined to fail.

Sources:

Baglino, Michael J. 2022. *5 Anti-Christian Philosophers Who Ruined America.* Catholic365.com.

Krason, Stephen A. 2022. *The Left vs. Realities of Race in America.* The Catholic Social Science Review. Vol. 27. The Society of Catholic Social Scientists.

Krason, Stephen A. 2022. *Needed Now: An Organized Effort and Plan to Defeat the Left.* The Catholic Social Science Review. Vol. 27. The Society of Catholic Social Scientists.

For further discussion and research

Introduction

1. Who might be some secular philosophers other than those listed having a negative influence upon western society. Explain.

2. Design and interpret how might the political spectrum be perceived in an alternate way.

3. Describe some recent political events illustrating the philosophies Gramsci and Marcuse at play.

Part I:

Philosopher 1 - Antonio Gramsci

Chapter 4:

Gramsci and the Left Today

Antonio Francesco Gramsci is probably the best known communist theorist in the western world. As such, he is a highly regarded, and the most influential Italian Marxist philosopher of the 20th century. Statues of Gramsci are found at Italian Piazzas and train stations. Names of roads are named after him throughout Europe and Italy. As a harsh critic of Benito Mussolini and Fascism, he was imprisoned in 1926 until his death in 1937. It was in prison where he was most prolific in his writings.
[Martin 2023]

Essentially a journalist he become a leader of the communist party of Italy before his incarceration as a radical socialist agitator. Born in 1891 to a middle class family in Sardinia, Gramsci suffered from a form of tuberculosis of the spine in known as Pott's disease during his early childhood. Never properly treated, he developed a 'hunch back' and suffered from ill health throughout his life. He had six other brothers and sisters.

As a youngster, his father worked in the local civil service but was arrested for corruption and sentenced to prison. Antonio was bitter about what he considered to be an injustice against his father which was combined with a bitterness at the poverty existing throughout the southern Mezzogiorno region of Italy. His academic understanding of it all was a result of attendance at the University of Turin where he received a partial scholarship. From there, his socialist and communist leanings blossomed. His intelligence recognized, Gramsci was given a position as a journalist for the Partito Socialista Italiano [PSI] in Turino. Consequently and subsequently, he dropped out of the university for he found his calling. Eventually, the PSI split according to ideological factions and Gramsci emerged as a member of its central committee.

Benito Mussolini did not take a liking to it all as worker rebellions increased throughout Italy. A former socialist himself, Mussolini initiated a fascist movement to quell the growing movement of trade unionists, workers and peasants. It seemed a workers' revolution was imminent and it threatened his emerging nationalist control. It had an effect of radicalizing further the socialist leadership in Italy. While a journalist, Gramsci was sent to Moscow, Vienna and Rome. He became an admirer of both Stalin and Trotsky. There he honed in on Marxist theory and tactics leading to his election in the Italian Parliament. In opposition to big land owners and the business class, Gramsci's efforts became ever more a threat to the Mussolini regime and his fascist movement.

So what exactly was so threatening to the recently formed Italian state? One such construct was his theory of 'factory-based democracy'. That is, the state would be based on worker control and planning as opposed to a parliamentary political system. It would be an economically controlled state, through a collective labor process led by trade unionists rather than politically controlled. While in prison, his writings further expressed his philosophies and tactics. From Gramsci's "Prison Notebooks" one of the more significant positions referred to the sociological concept of 'cultural hegemony'. To

Gramsci this was assumed to be a common sense view of society whereby a socialist working class would replace their own cultural hegemony over the current capitalist cultural hegemony. It could only be logical to the people of Italy that socialism was the best way, so he thought.

'Cultural Hegemony' was his best known theory in which he describes how the capitalist ruling class maintains power in capitalist societies. They maintain power through its cultural institutions accepted by all and consequently accepted as common sense normal. As these institutions are culturally accepted, it is the economic force of these institutions that coerces its citizenry to conform and thus maintain the status quo. It is also that acceptance and entrenchment of a capitalist society's culture and moral base that violence was not necessary to maintain control. Being a Marxist, Gramsci also believed that all capitalist societies would eventually and inevitably turn socialist. But it wasn't happening. There needed to be another impetus for revolution. That was to create an alternative culture to the status quo of society. And where did that culture of European bourgeois society originate and get its support? None other than the Catholic Church. Again, to offset the dominant culture the working class needed to learn of an alternate culture. To create the Marxist socialist society destined in history required breaking down the Catholic Church and simultaneously develop an alternative morality. Then, if there were a socialist revolution and a violent one, national and local police forces would need to be weakened which brings us to contemporary tactics combined with cultural hegemony.

Today's socialist movement includes the critical attack upon local police forces and transformation of the military as part and parcel of that effort toward socialist support. Combine that with Gramsci's call for an alternative to Christian morality in the form of radical secular feminism, LBGTQ and the creation of our new sexual state. Add the Black Lives Matter movement and Critical Race Theory imposed by the dictatorship of the curriculum specialists. Local and national forces would also have to be weakened when society reaches the Marxist theoretical stage of 'withering away of the state'. Then it will be the consent of the people which keeps society in tact rather that force. First, anarchy probably with the help of de-policing. Second, central governmental control by force. Third, governmental control giving way to people's consent and the cooperative economic state emerging. Communism accomplished. Silly, isn't it? Perhaps it is somewhat realistic for an emerging nation from the legacies of feudalism. How's about an advanced capitalist technologically based nation?

The centralized new sexual state is another interesting policy agenda of the left and supported by the Democrat Party of the U. S. Cultural breakdown is attained through deterioration of its Church supported mores. According to Jennifer Roback Morse [2018], the sexual state needs power in order to maintain control over its impossible objectives; that is, its propaganda of the sexual revolution. That sexual revolution beginning in the 1960s encouraged sex without marriage or commitment, abortion, divorce, sexual immorality of all kinds, and gender theories all in opposition to Christian teaching, the culture of the west. And so, sexual ideology is yet another excuse for centralized governmental control, Democrats all the way. Not specifically a Gramsci tool for counter hegemony, it is an outgrowth of his thinking nonetheless.

The working class would not only need to organize for revolution but also learn the intellectual folly of their capitalist and Christian society. Together with the propaganda stemming from the intellectual elite, the righteousness of a new morality would then further impel the revolution. Union struggle would not exist only for the improvement of labor, wage and living conditions.. It would exist for the transformation of society itself. So through media propaganda, the working class would learn an opposite all encompassing ideology to the current capitalist culture and ideology, even sexual mores. As an arm of the Democrat Party, today's media is accomplishing just that. A new culture and ideology emerges as icons of culture are torn down. The intelligentsia then rewrites the history of sport celebs, political leaders, historical pioneers, religious saints, celebrities on all levels. Christopher Columbus, St.

Juniper Serra, Thomas Jefferson, George Washington and our founding fathers, baseball, football players and coaches of the past; how's about John Wayne and more? Our woke NFL and NBA have caught on. New counter-cultural heroes are created - Gloria Steinem, Rue Paul, Che Guevara and Fidel Castro to name a very few. Young people just love to wear Che Guevara t-shirts as fashion today.

And if revolutionary efforts turned to violence, so be it. Revolutionary violence was justified, fascist violence not. As the intellectual propaganda machine moved the conservative forces more to the right, violence became more and more probable. The urban unrest of the past few years in such cities as Portland, Seattle, Minneapolis, New York, is especially telling of Gramsci's influence. Celebrities bail out the rioters as heroes. Burning down police stations are tolerated. Illegal demonstrations against Supreme Court judges are supported.

Many on the left in the United States are devotees of Gramsci. And the left in Europe give Gramsci credit for the Euro communism movement still prevalent through out the continent. If you watch the news, I don't think it is too much of a stretch to see that influence today. But applying any of Gramsci's call for an alternate cultural hegemony in Italy of the early 20th century is starkly divergent from an America of the 21st century. Can it really be put into practice and put into practice without everlasting damage to an advanced nation of 330 million?

Antonio Gramsci

Sources:

Gramsci, Antonio and David Forgacs [Ed.] 2001. *The Antonio Gramsci Reader: Selected Writings 1916 - 1935.* New York University Press.

Martin, James. 2023. *"Antonio Gramsci", The Stanford Encyclopedia of Philosophy.* Edward N. Zalta and Uri Nodelman [eds.]

Morse, Jennifer Roback. 2018. *The Sexual State: How Elite Ideologies are Destroying Lives and Why the Church Was Right All Along.* Charlotte, NC. Tan Books.

Chapter 5:

The Attack on Columbus: Gramsci All the Way

El Pub is a popular Cuban restaurant located on Calle Ocho in Little Havana, Miami. What stands out besides its great Latin American and Cuban food is a large mural depicting Christopher Columbus' arrival in what is now known as Hispanola, the Island containing the Dominican Republic and Haiti. It is there to honor this great explorer who was responsible for their presence and ongoing history in the Americas. Sadly, there has been reoccurring negative propaganda over the recent decades pertaining to the logic behind removing 'Columbus Day' as an official holiday with 'Indigenous Day'. Let it be clear:

Following Gramsci's directives, the left attacks America's first hero, Christopher Columbus and the Catholic church at the same time. Columbus was an Italian navigator from Genoa, Italy. He manifestly ventured out toward the so-called new world to accomplish three tasks: spread the Gospel of Jesus

Christ, acquire new riches for the Kingdom of Spain, and leave a lasting legacy for himself. He accomplished all three.

A devout Catholic, Columbus believed he was called to spread the Gospel: that as God sent Jesus into the world, Jesus has sent his disciples to proclaim him and to teach all nations in his name. Consequently, the Americas - north and south, are predominantly Christian in number and of a Christian based culture, including Native Americans.

Secondly, he sought increased riches, power and worldly status for Queen Isabella. This was certainly realized in a short period of time. But for us and more importantly in that process, we witness five centuries plus of an exchange of animals, plants, products and peoples from four continents. For example, and as a result, the Americas received such animals brought by Columbus himself: horses, cows, bulls, and sheep. What would the northern Native American culture be without horses? He supplied plants such as sugar, oranges and of course wheat, a main source of food for all the populace of these two continents – bread and pasta. In return Columbus and even more so, those who followed after him, brought to Europe and Africa corn, tomatoes, okra, potatoes, just to mention a few. Okra and corn prevented starvation in Africa until the 1900s while tomatoes and potatoes prevented starvation in Europe. The Germans and Irish can thus thank these explorers and more specifically the Incas for its new supply of potatoes, while Italians are indebted to the Incas for tomato sauce.

More significantly in today's era of identity politics, it was Christopher Columbus who initiated the exchange of Native Americans, African Americans and European Americans among four continents. It has taken over 500 years, but it is happening. Come to Miami or any major metropolitan community and you will see this multicultural Christian based society to which I refer. Europeans, Africans and Native Americans of all nationalities and ethnicities have migrated to all our major urban areas to create a mix of peoples never before seen in human history. Our emerging multicultural society requires a lengthy process and will require many more years and decades for it cannot be the ideal society we long for all at once. Thy Kingdom Come takes time.

We owe this and so much more to the efforts of the astronaut of his day, Christopher Columbus. The positive consequences of his ventures and those who followed far outweigh the negatives. Americans have discovered we live in and now a part of a multicultural world and multicultural society in the west. Well it has been developing for low these 500 years plus and all thanks to Christopher Columbus, his legacy.

As to the Knights of Columbus, the anti-Catholicism prevalent in today's political environment is never so clear as when Supreme Court Justice candidates are asked if they believe their Catholicism and membership in the Knights might interfere with any possible future decisions, or if they believe their religious beliefs keep them apart from the American mainstream. In addition, recent criticisms of the Knights include both 'imposing and proselytizing' and the fact that it is an all-male organization. [Kamala Harris] That they are anti-women because they are against abortion, and anti-

LGBTQ community for their opposition to gay marriage, that it is a racketeering organization because of its life insurance programs and policies. Such criticisms show both an ignorance of Catholicism and the many efforts of the Knights in helping the poor, the indigent, the lost, the crippled, the neglected and the homeless in our communities. Not to mention the all female and mixed gender membership groups throughout the church. A prejudicial judgment and discriminatory practice according to political ideology, this requires our steadfastness in standing up for our religion, beliefs, and religious rights against the left. Yes, this is Gramsci style tactics all the way.

Chapter 6:

Social Disorganization as a Way to a Centralized State

Jennifer Morse Roback maintains that the modern left is intent upon centralizing the American federal government via the promotion of deviant sexual culture. Let us count the ways.

But before we do, let's briefly summarize the Catholic view of sexual morality. One parameter is the need for modesty. The Catechism of the Catholic Church explains that modesty protects and encourages moderation in loving relationships. Even atheist Sigmund Freud called for the taming of excessiveness in sexual relations lest our culture descends into sexual anarchy. Perhaps a sexually repressed society but boundaries needed nonetheless. Given the need for moderation and temperance, the institution of marriage which is believed ordained by God, was established for that purpose. Marriage then is an institution of dignity for both partners, man and woman whereby modesty and temperance are maintained. Offenses against the dignity of marriage include adultery, divorce, polygamy, incest, cohabitation and any sexual acts before and outside of marriage. Children are the result of the marriage institution only, and at the same time, the child has the right to be respected from the moment of conception. This may be constraining to some but lies within the Christian tradition.

Now comes the sexual revolution promoted by and propagandized from the left. Sociologists have always connected the decline of society with promiscuity. Society was at its peak along with the restraint of sexual practice. The sexual revolution is one of traditionally moral reprehensible behavior now called progress. Ergo, the decline of society requires more governmental control. [Donahue, 2019]

Professor Roback shows us that the sexual revolution comes along and it becomes just another way for the central government to expand its control over personal lives. By expanding government expenditure and bureaucratic growth, it entrenches us within the administrative state. We become a sexual state.

What is purpose of the sexual state - to fulfill the purposes of the constitution? Protect people from fraud, provide for the common defense, insure domestic tranquility, promote the general welfare? NO - it is to give people the sex lives they want with minimal inconvenience. Want to have sex without having a baby? That's simple, the government will give you condoms at no cost. Don't want the baby you have with sex? That's no problem; we'll get you an abortion and we'll help pay for it. Want to have sex with someone you aren't married to? Easy, we'll get you a no fault divorce law and you won't be inconvenienced by having obligations to your spouse and children. And, want to have sex with someone of your own sex and still have a baby - no problem, we'll allow you to adopt or subsidize the technology needed to allow such, so as not to have any obligations to the natural parents. Voilà, our sexual state is in tact and the federal government expands in the process. The church has no legal say in the matter and the concomitant propaganda works against it all.

And what of deviance in general? [Henderschott, 2002]. Religion has always been a regulatory force for society. But the left now targets the moral majority as decadent. The church is too judgemental and intolerant they say. The church calls for personal responsibility. The government calls drug abuse a disease and provides the drugs for free. Pedophilia is now called inter-generational intimacy. Bestiality is now called inter-species communication, removing its deviant stigmas for both. Laws are made to protect. Suicide, once a sin is now an option for one's life whereby an individual may take upon themselves to die at a moment of their own choosing [a proposal of Herbert Marcuse, see chapter 7]. Growth, maturity and responsibility as a rational model for traditional values of family, work and community are now considered old fashioned and right wing. And so, crime is decriminalized, those guilty of misdemeanors and even some felonies are released from jail. Politicians, sociologists and psychologists define deviance, no longer priests and ministers. The concepts of sin and salvation are rejected. Let the state determine deviancy and administer its consequences.

The growth of our government is rooted in the theories of socialism, especially those of Karl Marx [see chapter 13]. Many over the years would witness the growth of 'creeping socialism', that is, a government of bureaucracy slowing inching forward toward societal control. Part and parcel of this movement is the promotion of class warfare and the engendering of personal envy. The decrying of capitalism and disparity of wealth accumulation is its main focus of this counter ideology. Marxism is the philosophy of the government taking away from the rich and powerful via governmental confiscation through personal and class revenge and envy. Eventually this leads to violence, as envy always does.

How do we see it today? The call for a single payer health care system [Obama Care] takes control of over a sixth of our economy. Paying college tuition and student debt of millions of college students requires confiscating funds from hundreds of millions of Americans. Anne Henderschott noted in

The Politics of Envy [Henderschott, 2020] reminds us of Prime Minister of England's Margaret Thatcher's quote, " The problem with socialism is that eventually you run out of other people's money." You need big government to run out of other people's money. In the recent Supreme Court Case overturning Roe V. Wade, the Democrats would falsely claim that the decision took away abortion rights for citizens. No it did not. It took it away from the federal government imposing it on everyone. The states now have the ultimate authority on the matter. Why does that throw fear and anger into the Democrats? Again, it takes away central governmental authority, the essence of socialism. And so the secular religion of socialism continues to impose and create begrudgment, envy, and overall resentment toward those of success and material gain. It is a philosophy of the material world only. Why when the Sandinistas overtook the government of Nicaragua, the first thing they did was confiscate the best homes for themselves. When President Nixon would visit Prime Minister Brezhnev of the U.S.S.R. he would bring along with him yet another Mercedes Benz as a personal gift, Brezhnev's favorite car. I think he ended up with six or seven. Be that as it may, every communist country has never become materially wealthy, save for China. But that is not because of Marxism; it is because of western investment, another story.

Sources:

Donahue, Bill. 2019. *Common sense Catholicism: How to Resolve Our Cultural Crisis.* San Francisco: Ignatius Press.

Henderschott, Anne. 2002. *The Politics of Deviance.* San Francisco: Encounter Books.

Henderschott, Anne. 2020. *The Politics of Envy.* Manchester, NH: Crisis Publications.

Morse, Jennifer Roback. 2018. *The Sexual State: How Elite Ideologies are Destroying Lives and Why the Church Was Right All Along.* Charlotte, NC. Tan Books.

For further discussion and research

Part I - Gramsci

1. Appraise any other American heroes or institutions attacked , vilified and slandered all for political purposes.

2. Survey the influence of the LBGTQ agenda in western society; pro and con. Give examples.

Part II:

Philosopher 2 - Herbert Marcuse

Chapter 7:

Herbert Marcuse and the Left Today

Herbert Marcuse was born of a wealthy German Jewish family in Berlin, 1898. Though not religious, he identified as a Jew ethnically. Yet, he did not personally experience prejudice during his youth. While in the German military, he began studying Marxism since being sympathetic Marx's ideas. But as to the current Marxist view, he could not identify with any major leftist political groups of his day.

Marcuse was an associate of philosopher Martin Heidegger. Heidegger eventually became a National Socialist [Nazi] and it impelled Marcuse to end their friendship. After the National Socialists gained power, Marcuse was forced to move to Holland and then to the United States.

Art and aestheticism was the original interest of Marcuse as a philosopher. He believed sculpture, painting, music and literature were useful in their teaching of philosophy, values and morals. It soon became for Marcuse, how could art aid Marxism in the revolutionary transformation of society. A humanist at heart, he now realized why he could not identify with German political leftists who were too structured in economics. No longer would Marxist revolution be confined to class struggle but also to human liberation. So he had to find another way, another key to revolution. This was critical social theory, applied today as critical race theory. And that is to expose western society as both repressive of our humanity and of its contradictions. Thus, while existing within our repressive state, social contradictions such as the rich getting richer and poor getting poorer are also maintained. Today BLM focuses on the oppressed Afro American community all brought about by an exploitative capitalist class. Or that the belief of unbridled competition as a positive contradicts with large scale corporations buying out their competition. This is their challenge in informing, teaching, propagandizing the populace and bringing it all to consciousness. Then the people's individual and subjective consciousness would impel the revolution forward. Thus not only the working class, but also the suburban housewife, the independent professional, and entreprencurs of all kinds would support the revolution out of compassion and justice for all. If not, rig the elections, change the rules midstream.

Similar to Gramsci, Marcuse was not in support of the administrative state. Actually, he feared its imminence. This is where he departs from his contemporary Marxists and the experience of the Soviet Union. Thus, he envisaged a 'one dimensional man' emerging, as opposed to the artistic freeing of his soul. It becomes mass conformity in a mass society. The bureaucratic state maintains repression and stifles individual desires of man. Bureaucracies dominate society while growing according to its own rationalizations and its interests. Its prominence overshadow of the individual. Not much different from the insights of German sociologist Max Weber. So we see current rebellion as a tendency toward bureaucratic growth of government and corporation combined with the refusal to work within these organizations and protestations of corporate profit making. We see a rebellious spirit directed toward the structure of western society as well as the intentions to liberate us from its restraints.

Admirable perhaps, but how effective or even realistic? In order to fulfill these contradictions inherent in repression, society would need to more equitably distribute resources, an equality of economic being. Equity. We hear that word all the time. It is not necessary equality, but rather represents the concept of fair and just distributions from the wealthy to the working class. This for Marcuse allows for the artistic flourishing of humanity. For we really live within a society of democratic unfreedom. Those who are one dimensional accept it, and those who are two dimensional criticize it, ie. Critical theory.

As to feminism, Marcuse believed it to be the most important and radical movement in the revolutionary process. Even radical to the point of replacing masculinity as too brutish and violent. Toxic masculinity is the call of today. He even supported androgyny often depicted as satanist by the Christian church. He believed it key to the destruction of capitalist society. Finally, unlike the secular left today, Marcuse was an ardent supporter of Israel.

Source:

Farr, Arnold. 2012. "Herbert Marcuse" *The Stanford Encyclopedia of Philosophy*. Edward N. Zalta.

Marcuse, Herbert. 1968. *One Dimensional Man*. Boston: Beacon Press.

Herbert Marcuse

Chapter 8:

Professional Revolutionaries in the U. S.

Psalms 2: 1
"Why do the nations conspire and the peoples plot in vain?"

Acts 5: 29
"Then Peter and the other apostles answered and said, We ought to obey God rather than men."

This is a young Christian's 1st hand witness to planned anarchy and destruction. The debates were intense. The doctrinaire logic of the various socialist ideologies was impeccable: Maoist, Trotskyist, Leninist, Marxist, Social Democrat of different shades, and it seemed true believers each and every one. The political correctness of its day.

This was the intellectual atmosphere in and around the University of Minnesota, Minneapolis in the 1960s from the campus itself, to the West Bank, to north and south Minneapolis where its Native Indian and Afro American populations resided. This naive young Catholic, with social justice concerns, did not realize what he was getting himself into. My understanding is that from the 1930s and most probably before then, Minneapolis was a hotbed of socialist ideas and movements. Whether on the street corners or in the bars of 'the west bank' [a notorious radical community], these were the ideas discussed, both enlightening and deceiving at the same time. The participating organizations were as follows:

SDS, Students for a Democratic Society
WEB Dubois Society
CPUSA, Communist Party of the United States
SLP, Socialist Labor Party
SWP, Socialist Workers Party
PLP, Progressive Labor Party
SNCC, Student Non-Violent Coordinating Committee
BPP, Black Panther Party

Proverbs 24:21-22 My son, fear the LORD and the king; Do
not associate with those given to change;
For their calamity will rise suddenly, And who knows the ruin
those two can bring?"
As a witness and participant in this 1960s student leftist era, I can attest to the involvement of

professional revolutionaries from each and every one of these organizations in planning and directing protests, marches and sometimes violent confrontations in order to build a social movement toward a socialist society. Oh yes, we were a naïve and provincial group of young Americans, many Christians, seduced by ideas we had never heard before. What a way to view things, how interesting, how mind expanding, along with the drugs fed us through the various grapevines. Our protests revolved around the selective service, Vietnam war, police oppression, racism, and of course capitalism itself. Christians yes, but just holding on by a thread. You know, as the old adage goes, if you believe nothing, you'll believe in anything. Well, universities have the greatest secularizing influence on young people and so they fell for it. What comes 'round, goes round' and history repeats itself. As there were a number of social movement events and protests intermittently approaching, meetings would take place at various campus or adjacent to campus locations.

Led by none other than members of any of the above groups but especially it seemed the Socialist Workers Party. They even had presidential and vice-presidential candidates on the Minnesota ballot and many other states throughout the country. One such state was California where the Chicano movement was quite outspoken and influential. I suppose this was an outgrowth of the Cesar Chavez Farm Workers Union though very few ever considered him communist. He himself was opposed to illegal immigration since such immigrants took jobs away from the local California migrant worker community which he was trying to unionize. He was a very religious Catholic and appeared loyal to America and the state of California.

So to continue, seems many of the speakers from the SWP were Chicano women from California. Good looking too. At that time there were very few Hispanics in Minnesota. Why mention this? Interestingly, the word around the young leftist community was - be careful of the Trotskyite women; they lure you into bed and then try to bring you over to the party line. LoL! And lure they tried.

But there were also young professional looking, well educated men who presented intelligent talks and outlines of the planned events and tactics involved. As part of the presentations were future intentions, and it seemed all above board visions. Their visions were not only of their Marxist utopia but also short ranged intentions of organizing students and workers. These people did not have jobs but rather involved full time with their party, and even offered others present to work as salaried community organizers for that purpose. Does the name Barak Obama sound familiar? There was a detail of procedure to take place during the demonstrations. They indicated specifically how to confront the police, how to both elicit and instigate violent police behavior, and how to respond.

"Romans 13:1" Let every soul be subject unto the higher powers. For there is no power but of God: the powers that be are ordained of God."

This brings us to Minneapolis today. The minority populations have grown substantially, many migrating from Central America and Chicago. Now for a little editorializing. I don't see the Hispanic population involved in these riots today in Minneapolis. They came here to escape such tyranny. They like their jobs. And these riots are not based around social justice but rather social discord and disruption. It is a Leninist tactic to create chaos and government response to further radicalize the local population, as per Socialist Workers Party meetings. They'll be the government in power eventually, whether by hook or by crook, it doesn't matter. Ideologically to them it is the destiny of the left, the providence of history. I believe it is up to us, along with prayer to guide us and not to let it happen. If we do believe, we can't fall for such nonsense. Gotta spread the word more!

"Hebrews 12:14" Pursue peace with all *people,*
and
holiness, without which no one will see the Lord."

My conclusion once again in life is that Christianity is anti-ideological. Ideologies fall by the wayside. Christianity cuts through all sides of ideology with clarity and truth.

Source:

Adapted from Baglino, Michael J. 2022. "Are there Professional Revolutionaries in the U. S.?" *More From a Florida Catholic*. San Francisco: Penguin Writers.

Chapter 9:

Critical Race Theory and the Marxist Putcsh

We hear of what Dr. Thomas Sergiovanni, Ph. D. used to warn America about back in the early 1970s; that is, the coming dictatorship of the curriculum specialists. Well it's here now and the battle is heating up between these curriculum dictators and American parents. Gender ideology and Critical Race Theory [CRT] are two major current curriculum impositions into our public schools. Right off the top I'll say, let us get our children out of the public schools and into private Christian and Catholic schools to save this country.

Now, as to Critical Race Theory [CRT], this is an academic approach of insisting of the connections between race, racism and power in America. It is a Marxist social construct that challenges the very foundation of the American order and our constitution. Everything to these neo-Marxists [progressivism/communism] is founded upon race. Since race is the most significant part of American lives, they say, there are outcomes in our society both legally and economically that are unequal. This ultimate inequity is the result of this unjust society and so must be transformed. One important note. The word communist is never used by liberals and progressives since it has always had a negative connotation in America and repelling to most. Therefore, though never used, it is exactly what Marxism is, from Karl Marx the father of communism, an authoritarian atheistic ideology toward political, economic and social control.

Transformation of our society would then come through the systematic attack on American institutions, its culture and heroes. Antonio Gramsci, a subject in this book, is probably the most influential European social and economic theorist of the 20th century. Gramsci is one of the Black Lives Matter [BLM] leaders' intellectual godfathers. He is referred to as a neo-Marxist by proclaiming his opposition to capitalism and supporting public ownership of wealth and property. Since capitalist societies are controlled by ideology and cultural means, Gramsci called for the systematic attack on its ideology and breakdown of its culture. This includes an attack on

Christianity which Gramsci believed the glue of the culture. Only this could alter the people's consciousness and thus pave the way toward the progressive civil society they envision.

Similarly, another subject of this book, Herbert Marcuse is a German atheist philosopher with profound influence upon BLM and the CRT mindset. Marcuse maintained that both continents, Europe and especially the United States were actually repressive societies - politically, economically, humanistically and sexually, and called for freedom seeking youth to rebel against it. This included criticism of the foundation of its culture, Christianity. He called for the disaffected and alienated to unite en mass against the prevailing structure. Funding of both activist groups and curriculum efforts by the like of George Soros, other leftist billionaires and leftist organizations, and tax funded governments ignite their movement.

How does the change evolve? Through college admission policies with race-based criteria; through curriculum guidelines in the public schools; by reinterpreting and rewriting the history by which we have been originally taught; by supporting anti racism activism like BLM; by funding such programs through corporate and government sources; by defunding the police and replacing them with mental health officers; by propaganda efforts in attacking so called racists, that includes Christians.

Lots of problems with all of this, especially for those of a Christian background. Seems Frederick Douglass and Martin Luther King, Jr. both based their civil rights efforts on the Christian vision of the human person as expressed in the U. S. Constitution. CRT also opposes the U. S. Constitution. It opposes nuclear families of a mother and father. It supports gay rights and marriage, legalized abortion, legalized drugs and prostitution.

CRT calls itself anti-racist yet advocates for cruelty and discrimination against white people. They say present discrimination is necessary to end past discrimination. I mean who would believe convoluted illogic and irrationalisms? The alienated, the misinformed, the anti-Christian forces of the centuries, that's who. Marxism has moved on from its assertion of an oppressed working class to oppressed minorities of non-white races. Success does not come from Christian values; it comes from white privilege.

And so, identity politics becomes of major importance. These Marxist academics will then give support to Black Lives Matter [BLM] who attempt to force awareness of this inequity through propaganda and urban turmoil. Bring racism into the consciousness of the American people and then force change from their guilt. Give support to CRT to promote the change through our youth. Force their social experimentation upon our nation and through it's youth is a better way to put it. And an experimentation it is, as Marxism works nowhere in human history. 'Thy Kingdom Come' takes time, not through violent revolution.

Source:

"Fighting Critical Theory." October, 2021. *CatholicVote.Org.*

For further discussion and research

Part II - Marcuse

1. Recognize the major players in financing and foaming domestic unrest in 21st century American. Explain their strategies.

2. Describe and evaluate some conflicts that have arrived out of the imposition of CRT in our schools.

3. Analyze the Hollywood production of *'Joker'* and its relation to contemporary social unrest.

PART III:

Philosopher 3 - Georg Hegel

Chapter 10:

Georg Hegel and the Left Today

Matthew 22: 21 "Therefore render to Caesar the things that are Caesar's, and to God the things that are God's."

1 Peter 2: 17 "Honor everyone. Love the brotherhood. Fear God. Honor the emperor."

He was born in Stuttgart, Germany in 1770 and published mostly in the early 19th century. One of the founders of western philosophy, inspired by the French Revolution, Phenomenology of Spirit was his opus on society, religion and consciousness. A onetime Christian and European philosopher, Georg Hegel [again, pronounced Geh-org Haygul BTW] proclaimed it was man's experience within society that allowed a consciousness to develop, nowhere else. His perception of self was intrinsically connected with the perceptions of others upon his self, a precursor to social interactionist theory. And his interaction with others' perceptions allows his own sense of self to become real. Through this experience, he is led to the recognition of this own soul. So that to Hegel, religion was a mode of consciousness of soul that sought to establish the truth of the relationship between man and God. And this consciousness could not exist without the state organized for the sake of man. Existential within the state. A liberal Christian, admitting to be a Lutheran, Hegel also saw himself as a liberal Prussian. That is, a political liberal who would support the Prussian state as long as it pursued the political ends of liberal Protestant humanism - the state organized for the sake of man. As his thinking progressed, it became that the incarnation and resurrection of Jesus was no longer within his belief system. Those beliefs did not come from society. The state was the ultimate authority and society the only arbiter of consciousness; thus, from a liberal Christian to a reborn atheist. [Redding, 2020]

Given this view, Hegel was ultimately authoritarian. The individual had no right contrary to the authority of the state. Since his consciousness emerges from his experience with the state, an integral part of the community, it is ultimately from the state whereby he draws his entire physical, intellectual, moral, and even spiritual life. All independent wills and rights are dependent on the existence of the state. The state is the highest morality, higher than society, higher than the family, higher than the individual. His tendency toward autocracy is such that social morality, not spiritual morality is the limits of man's consciousness. Freedom yes, but only within the bounds of state needs and control. With this his militant atheism grew. National and global statism was eventually the goal for all societies. All individual rights and freedoms would ultimately be subjected to societal and state structures.

Georg Hegel was essentially a philosopher of history and his dialectic of thought later was borrowed by Karl Marx. Though he did not coin or use the following terms, this structure of logic was essential: thesis, antithesis, and synthesis. That is as power relations in history led to conflicts or contradiction, thesis vs. antithesis, a new relationship would evolve, synthesis, thus overcoming the conflict or contradiction. The spirit or mood of the time is referred to a 'zeitgeist' and to Hegel, the zeitgeist of history, philosophy and society was in perpetual motion. History logically evolved from this perpetual zeitgeist. The synthesis eventually appearing brought society one step further. And so it was Karl Marx who when borrowing this concept viewed the mid 19th century zeitgeist as capitalism and its ruling class being contradictory to the needs of the proletariat, or working class. This would bring on its logical emergence of communism, a synthesis. [see chapter 14] The logical emergence of communism would not only be through historical processes but through a persistent systematic challenge brought on by social activists - unions, media, technocrats, politicians and intellectuals.

Jump to the 2020s with the worldwide and national rise in Marxist thought, arrives the so called 'Great Global Reset'. The Great Reset is nothing less than corporate socialism or communist capitalism on a worldwide scale. And adherence to the global structural changes is referred to as woke-ism. Go woke or else is the cry from the yearly meetings of the World Economic Forum which meets in Davos, Switzerland. American representative John Kerry at the most recent meeting assured the conference that the United State is totally cooperative with all its agendas including climate change financing, economic restructuring and centralization of governmental structures. This is especially with the election of its latest president, President Joe Biden. He assured them that President Biden was on board.

What is this exactly? None other than capitalism with Chinese characteristics, and let all other gods bow before it. For how is it that China is the only successful communist country? It is a Marxist socialist political economy funded by capitalist economic development, the reverse of the American system. The American system is one funded by capitalist economic development now implementing authoritarian state intervention with authoritarian measures to control the population. The Democrat Party is that party of Covid-19 nationwide restrictions, sexual state legislation and taxation regulations for large scale corporations, along with the destruction of small business. The middle class pays for it all. It is becoming a two-tiered system like China, an authoritarian centralized government at the top along with multinational corporations at the top and those at the bottom living a socialist life. They live their socialist life through the welfare initiatives of the Democrat Party. With the technology industry in its pocket, such welfare initiative now easier to manage include national medicare, a single payer health care system, free college tuition and free legalized drugs. Little do they realize that without God, all dictatorships whether national or global are doomed to failure. So which is your ultimate authority, God or the state? I think we are in for trouble. Watch out! What shall we do? Reread biblical quotes above. 'Thy kingdom come; they will be done' emerges too.

Sources:

"Why Hegel Knew There Would be Days Like These." *Hegel View on State and Civil Society*. Article1000.com

Rectenwald, Michael. Dec. 2021. "What is the Great Reset?" *Imprimus*.

Redding, Paul, "Georg Wilhelm Friedrich Hegel", *The Stanford Encyclopedia of Philosophy* (Winter 2020 Edition), Edward N. Zalta (ed.)

Chapter 11:

Are So Called Liberals Today Really Liberal?

When I think of liberal, I think of the era of Enlightenment, 18th century foundations of western democracies. I think of philosophers John Locke and Adam Smith, classic liberals who influenced the likes of Alexander Hamilton, James Madison and Thomas Jefferson. John Locke was the philosopher of life, liberty and the pursuit of happiness and of reason and tolerance. To Locke we needed to create a civil society, a social contract in order to resolve conflicts in a civil way. This is because he believed that the bible was in full agreement with human reason. Christianity, not atheism was necessary for the social order and atheism would lead to chaos. God was the source of all human energy and behavior.

We needed a government whereby no one was granted too much power. Our constitution outlined a government of limited powers given to the elected, that is a separation of powers each with checks and balances to insure that limited power - legislative, judicial and executive.

Adam Smith believed that human behavior was a consequence of a certain propensity in human nature, the propensity to trade and exchange for mutual benefit. People act according to their own interest and this in itself works in the interest of others. And here too there needed to be limits to government since it was a hindrance to economic progress. Economic progress for both Locke and Smith depended on non-interference of government, ie. capitalism and entrepreneurship the free market economy guided by the 'invisible hand' of supply and demand.

So liberals have always been pro capitalism as the only way to lift people out of poverty. Yes, government can help and play an additional role, but never opposed to capitalism. Not so with so called liberal Democrats, especially its progressive wing. Centralized government control and regulations are its major agendas.

Similar to enlightenment thinkers, liberals have always appreciated our Christian roots. Liberals today, and the leftists, are contemptuous of religion. And if they call themselves religious it becomes Judeo Christian thought with a liberal twinge; even a liberal dominance, not Christianity - a la Biden, Pelosi, Warnock. Oh, but they will support Islam, probably the most anti liberal religion around. I remember once reading psychoanalyst Carl Jung's evaluation of Adolph Hitler. He thinks like a Muslim and they think like him, he said. Case in point, Iran supported Germany in WWII.

2 Corinthians 11:13 "For such men are false apostles, deceitful workmen, disguising themselves as apostles of Christ."

Many in liberals circles today support segregation of the races. And if there is less than acceptable integration in their eyes, they support integration. Either, whenever it suits them. The superficiality of race replaces content of character as the determinant of social equality. They call this equity, the imposition of material equality and sameness upon all through higher taxation and distribution of income. Critical Race Theory suggests our racist society can only be remedied in no other way than this governmental imposition.

Liberals have always wanted to protect our sovereignty and borders. Liberals were opposed to illegal immigration in the 1960s since it took away jobs from Americans and threatened our sovereignty. Today they are for it. And since the 1990s, The North American Union became their cry. Canada, America and Mexico were to be one country and down with American nationalism. Mix up the tri-national working class. Class solidarity among the three nations became more important than national sovereignty and security. I am sure that when President Biden, Prime Minister Trudeau and President Andres Obrador met in January, 2023, this was their common perspective, to take the next step.

Open debate and dialogue, a liberal mainstay in our universities is no longer tolerated. Wokism, political correctness, conformity of thought are the catchwords for liberal ideological purity. Free speech is out. Conservative speakers banned and the curriculum itself controlled - critical race theory, gender ideology, Marxist propaganda.

Western civilization itself, bound in enlightenment philosophy is condemned as racist, sexist, violent, xenophobic. Yes, Western civilization, the most openly integrated society for all groups identified above, according to ones race, gender, sexual orientation, place of birth. In the 1960s, liberal President John F. Kennedy's policy of balanced budget, smaller government, lower taxes, free trade, anti-communism is the Republican policy today. Liberals today are for a larger and expanded role for central government, social engineering, higher taxes, increased the debt limit, and support for Cuba and Venezuela. Liberalism has come a long way and even George Orwell couldn't possibly think it would have gotten this bad.

Colossians 2:8 "See to it that no one takes you captive by philosophy and empty deceit, according to human tradition, according to the elemental spirits of the world, and not according to Christ."

Source:

Parsons, Talcott et. al. Editor. 1961. *Theories of Society*. New York: The Free Press.

Prager, Dennis. 2017. *Leftism is not Liberalism.* Townhall.

For further discussion and research

Part III - Hegel

1. Analyze the differences between the religious views of Hegel with Christianity.

2. Compare and Contrast capitalist liberalism with socialist liberalism.

Part IV

Philosopher 4 - Ludwig Feuerbach

Chapter 12:

Feuerbach and the Left Today

Next in the sequence of 19th century European philosophers is post Hegelian Ludwig Andreas Feuerbach [1804 - 1872]. Son of a religiously devout German Scholar, his writings had yet an additional influence upon Karl Marx. His movement away from medieval Christianity began in accordance with the the Protestant Revolution whereby it rejected clerical celibacy in an attempt to resolve the conflict between the spirit and the flesh. He also supported the vocation of the laity which today is inherent in Catholic practice. His belief was that the consciousness of spirit that exists was dependent upon the physical existence of human beings; pure spirit is nothing but the thinking activity of consciousness. Further, the attribution of God as a ruler, king, a merciful being are merely attributes of human nature and removed from the divine. [Harvey, 2011]

He was known primarily as an athiest and materialist since Feuerbach's view of religion became more philosophy as opposed to spirituality. This was due to the influence of pantheism, whereby God was not a personal God but impersonal distant from all of us. God was rather the physical universe constantly growing. To Christianity, the human form of God, or Jesus makes it opposed to pantheism.

Ludwig Feuerbach was a Lutheran, or should I say former Lutheran. He promoted his form of atheism as a contrast to what he believed the subjective projections of Christianity. Christianity to Feuerbach was created and originated out of the longings of humanity, not the longings of God. It was the needs of human nature that created religion. It was done this way: "You believe in love as a divine attribute because you yourself love; you believe that God is a wise, benevolent being because you know nothing better in yourself than benevolence and wisdom, and you believe that God exists, that therefore he is a subject – because you yourself exist, and are a subject." [DeBacksy, 2014] Since that be so, man could create his own philosophies and ethical principles based on human reason and logic. He need not rely on a man made superstition. Plus, along with economic development, human development could reach a potential accordingly. Religion therefore need no longer exist being an unnecessary man made creation and it is economics that can determine the limits of our potential. So at best, Feuerbach was pantheist, believing the universe was godly but there did not exist a personal godly being. And that many world religions encompassed its own projective notions of a god.

Consequently, Feuerbach became philosophically a materialist, and the world was composed of matter only. Our own consciousness was derived from this material world and nothing spiritual existed beyond it. In fact, our true humanity was restricted by religion, and our own consciousness was determined by the society in which we live. Ok. Karl Marx himself said Ok. And this is where Karl Marx departed from his philosophy. His ideas on religion and Christianity, as appealing to him as it was, was not sufficient to improve our society. We needed to act upon it in order to change it. As we hear from the left today, we are an integral part of our ensemble of human relations and see things from a historical and social context only. It is our existential reality. I repeat, our existential reality, the left's new mantra. Who we are and what we face within an economic superstructure: climate change, race relations, cultural and sexual identity, white privilege, economic opportunity, class conflict and relations, etc. From this point man is to organize, change and replace our existing social structure. University professors no longer educate but inspire action for change. We have an activist professorial class, activist judicial system, and activist bureaucratic agendas - local, state and federal.

Further, our consciousness is not just embedded within us from our interactions with society, the social structure and as Feuerbach calls it, our ensemble of human relations. It is taught to us by media, the communicative process of our communities. A precursor to Marshall McCluhan's *The Medium is the Message*, Feuerbach maintained societal information was communicated so as to impact meanings and perceptions of the world we lived in. The media of his day included newspapers, pamphlets, books, magazines, scholarly journals, neighborhood advertising. It was the role of the media to influence, reason and re-educate our existence. We note today the efforts of TV, internet, literature and cinema to do just that. Explore for yourselves the accusations upon CNN, MSNBC, Twitter, Facebook and the like. Propaganda and persuasion are easily recognized in the skewing, altering, eliminating and dishonest presentations of information. Ban President Trump on Twitter, or conservative pundits on Facebook. Paint the opposition as evil. Fail to report news of our broken borders and urban crime on CNN, accuse leaders of false collusion with Russia. Propaganda and the media are inseparable depending on the agenda. Yesterday the agenda was the status quo, today it is the socialist transformation and the global reset.

So, breaking down the faulty reasoning of religion being set, it is the changing our social existence that is to follow. Marx brings the anti Christian philosophies of Feuerbach to the next step. We work out what ideas are correct and incorrect so we can successfully alter reality in accordance with a revolutionary plan. Marx's socio-economic project is itself committed to communist revolution. Next chapters.

Source:

DeBakcsy, Dale. 2014. Ludwig Feuerbach. *Philosophy Now*.

Harvey, Van, 2011. "Ludwig Andreas Feuerbach", *The Stanford Encyclopedia of Philosophy*. Edward N. Zalta (ed.),

Ludwig Feuerbach

Chapter 13:

What Might Marxist University Professors be Responsible For? - An Eyewitness Account

What might Marxist university professors be responsible for? How's about ruining the nation of Venezuela and spying for Fidel Castro? Sounds kind of harsh, doesn't it? The general understanding of the damage done might be their propagandizing throughout the curriculum, even in high school. Or it might be the romanticizing of Marxist utopia to its students and then encouraging student riots, rebellions and overall academic mayhem without they themselves taking part. Students as slates to paint upon and tools for what they wouldn't do themselves nor have the courage for. That's for those American feminist professors. The dictatorship of the curriculum specialists in our public schools have been inching its way into our universities slowly but surely. Florida International University was on its way in the 1980s and I didn't even realize it.

Florida International University [FIU] is the state university of Florida at Miami. It is worlds apart from my provincial regional university in Minnesota, Winona State. FIU prides itself as uniquely different from others in the Florida state university system in both its globalist curriculum and majority of its faculty from outside the United States. It also considers itself a research university of renowned international professors, all well published and highly regarded in educational circles. I received my doctorate there. Two of my major professors considered themselves Marxist. Nothing unique here, but let's call them Prof. E. and Prof. A.

Professor E. was previously the Minister of Education of Venezuela and also Asst. Minister of Education in Spain. He specialized in International Development Education [IDE]. He gave me the responsibility of creating a Master's Degree program in IDE for FIU; that is, writing up course descriptions for the degree in the university catalogue. He wanted it fashioned after other universities that offered the program: Harvard, Stanford, UCLA, Columbia. So I researched those programs and replicated the major parameters. We created the degree program designed to train educators in planning educational systems in third world countries. He did that for Venezuela. In 1976 he designed the Venezuelan system according to Marxist ideology. We see the results of that today.

So, Professor E. and Professor A. sought out and recruited students, not only from South Florida but also Nicaragua, Panama, Costa Rica, Venezuela, Columbia, Guatemala and the Caribbean. Even Cuba. Somehow they were allowed in the 1980s and 90s.

Professor A., being a Cuban refugee himself, would visit Cuba to recruit. Simultaneously, he was a consultant for the Miami-Dade County Police Department. When he would visit Cuba, I suppose at some evening cocktail parties, representatives of the Cuban government would casually bring up the topic of the Miami Police Department. Professor A, ever the conversationalist and naively thrilled to be part of these international tête-à-têtes in his home country, probably spoke a little too much and to the wrong guy. Turned out he was speaking to a double agent and upon return to the U. S. was arrested and charged with spying for Fidel Castro. Such could not be tolerated during the Bush administration.

Being a student of the 60s and visiting Europe often, I had entertained leftist ideas and somewhat a part of the 60s youth movement. So when interacting with these guys while working on my doctorate, I certainly knew what they were talking about and knew where their sympathies lie. But I grew up. Professor A. was still naive as far as I could see, and Professor E. was a stickler on academic freedom. Seems the FBI gave him a hard time during his tenure at the University of Nebraska. They knew him. Miami at the time was not very tolerant of Marxism due to the large Cuban refugee population. Consequently, they were not outspoken about these ideas of theirs. Not like today. Nor were their courses taught overly ideological, but rather practical, focusing on the needs of the country as it developed economically. Good guys really, very professional. But this is what I remember most while at FIU and certainly learned a lot at my international university. Professor E. moved on to the University of Texas, now retired. Professor

A. was released from jail after a short stint. Now retired. Hope he kept his retirement benefits.

Related Sources:

Adapted from 2022 "What Might Marxist University Professors be Responsible For?" *More From a Florida Catholic.* The Penguin Writiers.

Baglino, Michael J. Doctoral Dissertation – 1992. "*Relevance of the Community College Curriculum to the International Student*;"
HYPERLINK http://digitalcommons.fiu.edu/etd/1368/"

For further discussion and research

Part IV - Feuerbach

1. Evaluate the role of modern technology in impacting meaning and perceptions in the world today.

2. Explain ways in which public school educators and college professors negatively influence our youth.

Part V:

Philosopher 5 - Karl Marx

Chapter 14:

Just What is Marxism Anyway?

Dialectical materialism, dictatorship of the proletariat, capitalist ruling class, revolutionary working class, class conflict, bourgeoisie, classless society. These are all terms emanating from the Communist Manifesto written by Karl Marx. They are repeated every day in the halls of congress and in the mainstream media. Well, not those exact terms, just the concepts they are associated with. These terms all have negative connotations in America, so they will use words like progressive, working people, white privilege, the rich and wealthy, equity, exploitation, cultural appropriation, critical race theory etc. All to help break down the standard cultural framework and economic structure. Marxism of the 21st century.

Born in 1818 from a Jewish family of 9 siblings, origins of his first anti-Christian inklings was the forcing of his attorney father to convert from Judaism in order to keep his job. As a professor himself, Karl Marx, due to political conditions in

Germany, his writings were considered too radical and threatening for its age and he was forced to continue his work in Paris, London and Brussels. And here it is, one of my more frequent college lectures; it's a classic outline for history and the future according to Karl Marx:

"The history of the world is the history of class struggle."

COMMUNISM [future centuries]

CAPITALISM [18th century and beyond]

FEUDALISM [Middle Ages]

SLAVERY [pre–Middle Ages]

Karl Marx, 19th century philosopher and economist maintained that the history of the world was a history of class struggle. That is, the Marxist theory adopted as the official philosophy of the Soviet Union [USSR], Chinese [CCP] and other communist countries. According to Marxism, political and historical events result from the conflict of social forces and are interpreted as a series of contradictions with their solutions emerge. The conflict is caused by material needs. He referred to this theory as 'dialectical materialism'. As material needs changed, so did the social and economic structure of society. Follow me here.

Each stage in history is based on the control of one class over the other, an exploitative relationship. The existing contradiction is described as a thesis versus an antithesis. Thus, slavery being an illogical institution, will leave the majority of people in material need. Though slave owners reap the benefits of their control [thesis], slaves are naturally opposed to this relationship of powerlessness and material want [antithesis]. Conflicts emerge and a new social order develops [synthesis]. That new social order according to Marx becomes feudalism.

Feudalism is the next stage in history whereby large landholders, lords and nobles, maintain control over its workers, serfs, for a meager wage. Not quite slavery but exploitative nonetheless. Pre industrialized Europe, Latin America and post slavery Brazil and America are examples. Again the contradictions of this relationship reaches its boiling point as serfs and indentured servants cannot improve their lot materially. Conflicts between land owners, servants and serfs arise to the point of social change once again as the existing relationships will not function. Combine this with a worldwide industrial revolution, forces are in play for new relationships to emerge. This new system is called capitalism.

Capitalism is the system emerging in Europe and the United States especially. These two continents proceed with industrial growth and wealth based on the capitalist ruling class dominating over their workers, or working class. Another way in which Marx referred this relationship is the owners of the means of production's exploitative control over the proletariat. The bourgeoisie are the middle class and small business owners who actually imitate the culture of the capitalist ruling class to help maintain the former's control. They live in the better neighborhoods, join the local country clubs, send their children to the better schools. The mass of workers, however, fuel their economic growth and wealth by their hard work while they remain relatively poor, just getting by. The only solution is the uniting of all workers mostly through union organization and revolt against the ruling class. Through violent revolution, they take control of all property and business emerging into a worker's paradise.

Capitalist ruling class
_____ = **violent revolution**
Proletariat working class

Sounds simple. It has never occurred in history. Rather, communist revolutions have only occurred in agrarian economies, those who have never developed industrially. Eventually, as hopefully these nations do develop, the growth of a centralized government keeps control and the workers maintain its cooperative management of all business and industry. Marx envisioned communist revolutions in advanced capitalist nations like Europe and the United States. A dictatorship would soon emerge, called 'the dictatorship of the proletariat'. It would last for a mere 20 years as the state eventually withers away. Large centralized bureaucratic governments are entrenched and do not wither away. Democrats know this and their increased budgeting of ever more government programs make sure the centralized state is expanded. Here in the U. S., since the unions have not emerged as the leaders of the revolution, leftism has become more of an intellectual challenge. The intelligentsia along with governmental bureaucracy have joined forces over both capitalists and workers by imposing their way. Through university training and media control, the message is getting out there. Joining forces with the centralized federal bureaucracy, their march continues.

Why is it imposed? Because Marx left a few things out. He did not foresee working people themselves owning stock on private business and corporations. He did not foresee professional athletes such as NBA, NFL, MLB, MLS ball players earning millions through the free market. He did not foresee the professional class growing in general and working classes living as comfortably as they do. So the media skews the perception. He did not foresee religion, especially Christianity continuing to make such a strong impact on western culture and around the world. He did not foresee race relations improving to the point of Christian brotherhood. So, they have to create more racial strife and disembowel the middle class. To Marx, Christianity was the enemy and all leftist forces attempt to destroy it. Christians owe their allegiance to God, not the state. Communists cannot have this. Leftists exacerbate ongoing racial and ethnic strife and believe such brotherhood must only exist within the socialist social structure. It is all about power and this ideology is their god, not the Father, the Son and the Holy Spirit.

Marx believed the history of the world is a history of class struggle by finally bringing all classes into one, a classless society. Make everyone the same, think the same within the centralized state [equity]. Capitalists believe that the history of the world is a history of freeing the means of production toward material abundance. Christianity believes that the history of the world is to lead man up toward God with God in control. Your choice.

Karl Marx

Communist Manifesto

Source:

Adapted from Baglino, Michael J. 2023. Just What is Marxism Anyway? *Europe Meets Florida*. LT Publishing.

Chapter 15:

What Factors Contribute to Economic Development?

Loved to pass on economic ideas to my students when at Miami Dade Community College, now Miami Dade College. Most of the foreign students in my classes were business majors, especially the Jamaicans, Nigerians, Brazilians and Pakistanis. Miami Dade College has the largest enrollment of foreign students than any other college and university in the U. S. Most were business majors and so many wanted to stay in the U. S. My dissertation showed that these students were pleased with the education they received. It was relevant to them even if they did return. They knew what I was talking about, and if they did remain here, I can't imagine that they wouldn't vote Republican. Not an economist by a long shot, but it was one of the topics in our required general social science course so I presented the material to them.

Developing countries know how difficult it is to overcome poverty. Even being blessed with natural resources is not enough of an aid toward development. They have to diversify. As mentioned, most of the students in my social science classes were from Asia, Africa, South America and the Caribbean. Their cultures were very traditional and most believed that the traditional ways and thinking of the homeland stifled economic growth. Women could not work in certain occupations, class distinctions were rigid, old ways of doing things were difficult to change.

In addition, many of these countries were ruled by authoritarian autocratic governments. These governments often spent more on military wants than on population needs, not to mention the corruption within those governments. Further, their populations were growing at rates outstripping gross national product rates making it difficult to maintain a growth pattern. Probably the biggest reason for stifled economic growth to many an economist and also to this author is the lack of transfer of capital to these countries. Vice President Kamala Harris keeps calling for finding the root causes of migration across U. S. borders. Easy, no economy can develop without capital to spur its development. They need the necessary factories, equipment, and tools required for modern production. Developing, growing nations do not produce migrating peoples looking for a better life. It is right there in their own countries. Finally, they need something called educational opportunity; i.e., a well-trained and educated workforce to increase economic productivity. Schools train the populace with the skills needed and universities train the populace for management responsibilities for corresponding industries. It's land and resources, labor, capital and management appropriately coordinated.

So what factors are required to contribute to economic development? What are the learned lessons over the centuries now that the world is in a global mode of development?

Firstly, an economically developing society requires agricultural productivity on a mass scale. Subsistence farming is not going to carry the load. Mass agricultural productivity without big government hindrance and opening to worldwide markets can eliminate poverty and stimulate this segment of a nation's economy.

No factor contributing to economic development is more significant than capital accumulation either through trade or investment. Encouraging foreign investment is required. It is foreign investment which spurred on growth in Vietnam, Singapore, South Korea, Mexico, India, Brazil and of course China. Communism didn't do it. Plus, grants, loans and technology transfer is provided by international organizations such as the World Bank and International Monetary Fund [IMF]. Loans can be used for infrastructure, roads, power plants. Directives in IMF policy can influence reductions in government spending to keep the budget balanced or sometime increase government spending for health and welfare programs. Similarly, regional organizations such as the Organization of American States [OAS] or African Development Bank can do the same.

Hindrances to buy and sell in the market place need to be removed. Capitalism, not government control is the motivating force to stir up the economy. Secure banking and monetary systems in these countries can assure the supply and demand currents necessary for growth. Global centralization govern of mental control toward economic development is now the popular view in solving global economic problems. Called the 'Global Reset', organizations mentioned above [IMF, World Bank, OAS] are calling for more influence upon national governments. Managed capitalist economies on the order of China and India is their model.

Economist Peter Rodriguez [2010] clearly explained the experiences of these two giants in changing course toward the 21st century. China, being a command economy, was lagging behind Europe and Asian tigers of the 20th century. Chinese leaders, especially Deng Xiaoping, called for a change and to alter their course in policy. He gave incentive for farmers and business community members alike all while investing in China's infrastructure. He invited capital from the outside. The experience in India was also one of opening the economy to allow India to trade more freely in the world. India was also blessed by the influx of technology and capital from its own emigre citizens. Upon visiting western nations, they themselves would send back money and knowledge to their home country and spur on new high-tech industries now characterizing the Indian economy.

Since the world markets are now more connected and integrated, managed global growth appears to be the future. What happens in one economic sphere will automatically effect another sphere. At the same time let flourish more opening toward increased trade, buying and selling in the marketplace, and less government taxation, limitations and restrictions to allow entrepreneurial efforts to succeed. Controlled management indeed.

Successful economies are those where people receive incentive for being more productive. Governments need to let go and allow the populace their freedom to produce. Yet at the same time governments can fund investments themselves, invite capital and even eliminate their own corruption. On a worldwide scale, a daunting effort.

Source:

Antell, Gerson and Walter Harris. 2005. *Economic Institutions and Analysis, 4th ed.* New York: Amsco Publications.

Baglino, Michael.1992. *Relevance of the Community College Curriculum to the InternationalStudent.* digitalcommons.fiu.edu/etd/1368/"

Rodriguez, Peter. 2010. *Why Economies Rise or Fall.* The Great Courses.

Chapter 16:

Marx's Communism via Marcuse: New Millennium Style

After Donald Trump entered the presidency and began his activist style of leadership, it hit me. America spoke up, thus stemming the tide of our decreasing sovereignty and new millennium communism into the U. S. Or so I thought. Sociologists for decades have indicated that communism would or could come to America in every way but in name only. So let's just call this Democrat Party push excessive administrative growth, propaganda and control. The clearest example of that is the collusion between media and government, a propaganda machine similar to the CNN, MSNBC vortex, not unlike the Soviet Union, Communist China, North Korea, Cuba, Vietnam, etc. Portrayed in films and books like Fahrenheit 451 & 1984, Marxism collides with almost every principle of western civilization and American life - true liberalism. The attack on our sovereignty, capitalism and Christian morality was the hallmark of the Obama administration and his followers, but

Marxism fails everywhere. Our way - not perfect, but it is better.

And so, since the 2020 election, we have seen our communism coming to America in every way but in name only. So many were shocked and dismayed that President Trump was defeated by Joe Biden. The 24/7 four year attack on him was nothing less that psychopathic, twisting anything they find. Incessantly accused but never found guilty. They ranted and raved against a man that had the courage to stand up to them. President Trump himself underestimated their strength and intentions. They were on their way to the socialist dream but he stood in the way. So the mess we see now is a showcase of what is to come should they remain, worse and worse and worse. As of this writing, the FBI just invaded the home of President Trump. This is yet but another tactic to retaliate against the so-called reactionaries as witnessed during and after the revolutions in Russia and China. The movement of communism, now called progressivism, part and parcel with the global reset, is an attempt toward a worldwide dictatorship of corporate, government, media and technocrat collusion. In the model of China for the whole world, it is destined to fail. The leftists believe themselves that this global reset cannot succeed without the United States; thus this attempt at radical change. Two things stand in their way, The United States, Israel and worldwide Christianity, especially the Catholic Church. So here we are today - our existential threat and spiritual war.

The following is borrowed from our two anti-Christian philosophers, Gramsci and Marcuse. [Marcuse, 1968] What then becomes the purpose of large-scale organizations, whether they be corporate or governmental? The administrative state must convince citizens:

1. think that they are freer than they really are, sexual freedom;

2. provide the citizens with enough goods to keep them pacified, the social welfare state, legalized and even free drugs;

3. promote identifying with the alternate administrative state as opposed to their capitalist oppressors;

4. to eliminate political discourse as the politics desired have arrived.

A socialist administrative state [which appears to already exist] must reveal what are the contradictions of capitalist society and invoke social change. Otherwise, the oppressed identifies with the oppressor. People must see that they actually live under a sense of false unity. Watching the same TV shows or identifying with the same sports teams, or slogans like the 'American people', or the 'American way of life' are different for a diverse population like ours. This is especially so between the rich and the poor. There is no reason to identify with the oppressor under these circumstances. Critical thinking becomes criticism of the society they live in. It is not really critical thinking any longer; it is being critical.

Marcuse [1965] also called for an intolerance of our social political framework. Whereas the revolutionary movement must call for tolerance among its opposition, the movement must maintain an intolerance toward the enemy's existence. Or what he refers to as 'repressive tolerance' a critique of pure tolerance. Common criticism of the left is their intolerance toward Christianity and its morality, capitalism and its ideology. This is a purposely designed construct of our university intelligentsia and curriculum specialists based on Marcuse's philosophy. They oppose tolerance toward the right purposely in their march forward to overcoming it. It is their strategy in overcoming. Thus, they won't be stopped until they are stopped. Compromise won't work.

Political correctness is part of that war. Every communist revolution has employed their own form of political correctness. Revolutionary leaders impose a purity of ideological thought superseding all other perspectives. This goes against everything the west has cherished for over 200 years. So much change, so many issues, so many perspectives, and so many existential realities to deal with them. We can view them from geographic, geo-political or internationalist vantage points; or from a sociological standpoint whether it be a conflict, symbolic interactionist or functionalist perspective. There are psychological perspectives such as psycho-dynamic, humanistic, cognitive, biological, behaviorist evaluations. Then the ever-intrusive economic influences – class, productivity, monetary and banking, business and government size, policy and growth perspectives. Suppose we grasp at some historical and anthropological insights, culture, leadership, evolutionary and social movements influences. They all have value, they all have elements of truth, they all can entertain issues at hand with some validity, none 100%. Yet, many have taken it upon themselves to impose singular, simplistic notions, that aggressive authoritarian impulse. It's the fear of freedom, makes their world secure. Political correctness then takes on a fundamentalist religious character. Plato said it, "the more you know, the more you realize you don't know." Kind of humbles you. Likewise, Aristotle once said, "It is the mark of an educated mind to be able to entertain a thought without accepting it." Political correctness does not allow it. They know it all already. All I really know is what my Catholic priest and Baltimore Catechism told me in grade school in 1950 – Our purpose on this planet is to know God, love God and do his will. The rest is all fleeting vanity. Political correctness does not allow that. They are the new Gods now, all for the state.

Source:

Farr, Arnold. 2012. "Herbert Marcuse" *The Stanford Encyclopedia of Philosophy*. Edward N. Zalta, Ed.

Marcuse, Herbert. 1965. "Repressive Tolerance" *A Critique of Pure Tolerance*. Boston: Beacon Press.

Marcuse, Herbert. 1968. *One Dimensional Man*. Boston: Beacon Press.

Solzhenitsyn, Alexander. *Gulag Archipelago: Abridged*. Harper and Row.

For further discussion and research

Part V - Marx

1. Criticize the Marxist states of Korea, Cuba and Vietnam as antithetical to Marx's communism.

2. Who is Alexandr Solzhenitsyn and summarize the contribution of Solzhenitsyn in our understanding of the Soviet Union's experiment with Marxism.

Part VI:
Philosopher 6 - Charles Darwin

Chapter 17:

Charles Darwin and the Left Today

You know Adolf Hitler was a socialist. The National Socialist Party had intentions of an administrative state in control and in cooperation with large scale business enterprises existing in Germany at the time. Its term in power emerged to include a propaganda machine the likes of which has been replicated in subsequent larger powers: Russia, China and the United States. Most notable propagandist in Nazi Germany was the infamous Joseph Goebbels, considered the founder of modern propaganda techniques. Goebbels was responsible for promoting Nazi ideology through the demonization of its enemies and at the same time appealing to the emotions of its constituents. Considered enemies of the day in Nazi Germany were communists, wealthy capitalists, Jews, Catholics, gypsy's, and homosexuals.

The propaganda machine which he created was not based on truth but rather only those so-called truths that supported their own ideology. And as

Goebbels often reiterated in close quarters, "if a lie is repeated enough, the people will begin to believe it." In support of this propaganda machine, demonstrations and riots were planned and organized in order to reinforce and increase the fervor of the state's intentions. Germany became an administrative state of totalitarian proportions. Nationalization of all industry, rewriting of history and culture, re-education within in all schools and vilification of resistant social groupings was its agenda. Newspapers and magazines, art and cinema became its propaganda outlets. The true authoritarian, totalitarian state.

So how does Charles Darwin fit into all of this? McNamara, 2021] Mostly known for his masterful work "On the Origin of Species", Charles Darwin originally wanted to become a medical doctor and then an Anglican minister. However, education at the University of Edinburgh and Cambridge influence him to take another direction as a geologist and biologist. Darwin's famous Theory of Biological Evolution stated that all species of organisms arise and develop through the natural selection of small, inherited variations that increase the individual's ability to compete, survive, and reproduce. His theories were developed mostly from his experience on the Galapagos Islands off the western coast of South America. In addition to these anthropological experiences, Darwin was strongly influenced by Thomas Malthus and his "Essay on the Principle of Population." According to Malthus, our world population was destined to increase geometrically thus overpopulating the world. How could people survive? They have been doing so throughout history via what Darwin later called natural selection and survival of the fittest and it would continue.

As a Christian, he eventually believed his evolutionary theory could be reconciled through Christianity as a sort of synthesis. His biological ideas became dominant in his mind. Theories of Social Darwinism eventually emerged. Christianity was obviously outdated, a similar recent view expressed by by Hillary Clinton: Christianity must conform to the times and our way of thinking. This overlaps with the Catholic church's conflict with the secular notion 'liberation theology', a neo-Marxist construct.

Darwinian theory of evolution is in direct opposition to creationist theory of various Christian religions found within Protestantism. The theory of Evolution relegates humans as similar and even equal to the animal kingdom in most aspects of biology. As suggested in chapter 1, a parallel position taken by many animals rights organization today, such as PETA. Furthermore, Darwin and his intellectual mentors believed it competition and survival of the fittest that motivates humans. And unlike Christianity, his secularizing theories viewed women as not equal to men in that evolution.

The principles established in Social Darwinism, a sociological construct, justify acts of racism, sexism and thoughts of ethnic superiority. Proponents argue certain human races and ethnic groups have desirable and strong traits. These groups dominate perceived weaker and flawed groups, and deserve dominion. In Europe, German leader and former socialist Adolph Hitler used the theory of Social Darwinism to declare the Aryan race supreme and others, particularly Jews and other minorities inferior.

Herbert Spencer, a 19th-century philosopher, receives credit for conceiving the theory of Social Darwinism. Spencer considered the government in Europe established by white races superior in technology, economy and structure to governments elsewhere in the world. Spencer stated natural selection played out in the military and economic dominance of European countries led by white rulers. The strong white race gained power while "inferior" races lagged behind. It justified colonialism and imperialism at the time, suggesting Asian, Black and Indigenous populations were not as capable as their European colonizers.

Left or right, totalitarianism is totalitarianism. All totalitarian states have used the same tactics to foster its ideologies: twisting history, twisting truth, demonizing its enemies, via nationwide propaganda.

Sources:

Allport, Gordon. 1954. *The Nature of Prejudice.* New York: Addison Wesley.

Baglino, Michael J. 2022. "5 Anti Christian Philosophers Who Ruined America." *More From a Florida Catholic.* San Francisco: Penguin Writer.

McNamara, Robert. 2021. "Biography of Charles Darwin: Originator of the Theory of Evolution." *www.Thoughtco.com*

Charles Darwin

Chapter 18:

Freedom, Determinism and Authority

Even Forest Gump contemplated the nature of life being a matter of freedom, determinism and by whose authority does one live. Are we all floating around as the feathers and taken up by the wind, or are we to seek our own destiny? Is it all a matter of chance or determination? Authoritarians are deterministic, in that our lives are determined by forces we cannot control. They fear freedom. Those who believe in freedom believe in personal choice to determine their lives. They take on a moral responsibility to where they lead themselves. To become the best version of themselves.

All philosophers presented in this book are deterministic and authoritarian. [Thiroux, 2009: 103 - 109] Georg Hegel was an historical and cultural determinist. He believed the cultural environment determined human perfection and this perfection could only be realized through cultural development in history. He called that perfection reaching 'the absolute mind' of this world. This was his view of God as he left his Christian roots. Create the ultimate state and you create the absolute perfected mind. New World Order.

Charles Darwin was a biological determinist. Animals survived only through the various processes of nature. Their existence within a given evolutionary stage determines their survival. Given the changing nature of the world at the time of dinosaurs, dinosaurs could not survive but rabbits could. As the world changed, dinosaurs could not adjust, rabbits could. Natural selection and survival were the result of strength, intelligence and what we have come to realize as genetic predispositions.

Ludwig Feuerbach, believing religion a man-made creation, his own thinking evolved toward social determinism. Our consciousness was determined by the society in which we lived, our status, our interactions, our vocations, our communities. Social consciousness was to be determined and reinforced by the social forces of power and the use of propaganda. Propaganda and persuasion would help create that ideal society in which we should be living. Ultimately this sounds similar to the above.

Karl Marx was an economic determinist. Class struggle was that social manifestation of economic exploitation. Human and social development would evolve from agrarian, feudalistic, capitalist and socialist stages in history. An emerging classless society was determined by historical forces and the creation of authoritarian government would help bring that about. It would last a mere 20 years. Did he ever hear of 'the deep state'? The nature of bureaucracy is that they try to hold on to their power and further expand for its own sake. See sociologist Max Weber on this one. Watch out for the coming New World Order.

Antonio Gramsci and Herbert Marcuse were neo-Marxist philosophers of the 20th century. Largely critical and nihilistic of the world we lived in, they did not hesitate to call for violent revolution from among the intelligentsia, the working class, the poor and the disenfranchised from around the world. Centralized authoritarian government and propaganda outlets would assure this outcome, worldwide.

We have come to realize that Sigmund Freud was a biological determinist and personally authoritarian. He hated anyone who disagreed with him. Our behaviors are determined by our genetic makeup and our true natures of sex and violence need to be repressed by society. He calls them inner drives and unconscious motivations. Calling for needs to be repressed led to behavioral psychology granting no spiritual nor humanistic nature to humanity - a la B. F. Skinner. Rather, by creating an environment of physical, cultural and social control would determine the kind of human we are striving to be. Behavior control techniques then become ubiquitous. Hello Hegel and Feurerbach again. Communism, Nazism and the administrative state are based on this psychology. OK in the classroom but emanating from Washington and Beijing it's hard to think so.

The difference between Christianity and other deterministic philosophies is one of individual choice. Though God may be all knowing [omniscient], all powerful [omnipotent], and present everywhere [omnipresent], he may know past, present and future in world history. Yet the nature of Christianity is that a follower of Christ must make that decision to follow Christ everyday. It is not imposed upon him and God would never do that Himself. So his own life in this sense is self determined, an agreement to obey His commandments and choose accordingly. A Christian believes it is our personal decisions which make us free within the body of Christ, to choose and become. Not from Washington, Moscow, Beijing or any large political center of the European Union.

All philosophers above - all deterministic, all authoritarian.

Source:

Thiroux, Jacques P. and Keith W. Krasemann. 2009. *Ethics: Theory and Practice*. Upper Saddle River, N. J.: Prentice Hall

For further discussion and research

Part VI - Darwin

1. Review and assess Social Darwinism in view of more contemporary biological, social and cultural research and phenomena.

2. How does Christianity debunk evolutionary theory?

Part VII:

Philosopher 7 - Sigmund Freud

Chapter 19:

Sigmund Freud and the Left Today

You might say, what does Sigmund Freud have to do with anything today since so many of his ideas were so far off. Well, he is referred to as the father of modern psychoanalysis and we can assign credit to his ideas on biological forces, neurological forces and cultural forces in behavior. We give him credit for the recognition of developmental psychology though I doubt children really are caught between the competitive love and hate of their parents. Psychology defined as the scientific study of mind, cognition and behavior, yet there is no scientific basis for any of his ideas. They are mostly philosophical. Fascinating as concepts ego, id, superego and libido might be, he never quite measured or specifically identified these theories or their origins. But he was a determinist, whereby he focused on our behaviors and personalities as controlled by forces entirely other than our free will. He correctly perceived patterns of behavior called defense mechanism: denial, projection, repression, rationalization, sublimation, reaction formation, displacement. Part and partial of such insights did allow counseling and clinical psychology to take leaps and bounds as a profession after his life and publications.

No, his far-reaching influence was more in the area of philosophy than psychology. The oldest of 8 children, Freud moved to Vienna from Czechoslovakia as a young child. Like Marx, Freud was an atheistic Jew with a great disdain for Christianity and Catholicism in particular. He viewed it as infantile thinking. He became a medical doctor focusing on neurology. Special influence was in the areas of childhood development, sexuality, dreams, personality and therapy. Spirituality in humans never existed to Freud as man was reduced to neurological, muscular and skeletal systems. And none of it survives after death. All of humanities' drives were instinctual, none spiritual. And so, to free and improve our being was to become more sexually free and less sexually repressed. As our secular world progressed, so did its anti-religious impulse. This thinking caught on. [Fromm, 1962]

It caught on not only in the general populace but among the intelligentsia who similarly viewed religion as a repressive influence on sexual fulfillment. As leftist propaganda increased, attacking pillars of Christian morality increased. And here is the important point of leftist strategies. Break down the moral pillars and you break down the cultural pillars of capitalist societies. Antonio Gramsci and Herbert Marcuse were those ideological thinkers calling for such moral and sexual rebellion. So comes the sexual revolution as a tool in the promotion of the world wide secular socialist agenda. And with it the contrary anti-Christian view on psychology and sexuality a la Sigmund Freud. What exactly is that philosophical position in leftist ideology as opposed to Christianity and Catholic Christianity?

Liberal and former CNN owner and executive Ted Turner, said it once in a TV interview, "Thou shall not commit adultery? Old fashioned thinking. We are beyond that. Why it's the end of the 20th century." Here you have it and while he was married to Jane Fonda. Our Christian-Judaeo culture of course sees it differently. God's laws are God's laws for eternity and disobeying God's laws are called sin. There are consequences for sin. Uh, oh! We don't want to hear that. Secular society doesn't want to hear that. Freud doesn't want to hear that. Freud himself had a great fear of the Catholic Church and would not visit Rome because the spectre of the Catholic Church haunted him. And I mentioned previously, he hated anyone who disagreed with him. Why even though he viewed homosexuality as arrested development of some sort, he did not say the behaviors associated with this condition was wrong or sinful. Here we have it again, the unbelief in sin.

America has always been a purposeful nation and purposeful populace. Commit to purpose, goals and direction or you'll be pushed around by every wind there is. And it is Christian psychology that calls us to commit to ideals and not Freud's world of the subconscious that determines one's life. To Christianity, the subconscious is the place of our fallen nature, the seven deadly sins: lust, gluttony, greed, sloth, wrath, envy, pride. Focus on our goals and God Himself with our faith, reason and will – not our instinct and impulse. Freud avoids such a perspective. And to the left where sin does not exist and there is no sin to admit, guilt is also avoided. So the modern approach is that fulfilling one's sexual desires leads to personal fulfillment rather than reaching one's purpose and goals through one's faith, reason and will. To become the best version of yourself. Oh, and temporal needs be taken care of by the government. Therefore, while we are at it, let's pay for their education, health, tuition, housing, food, legalize drugs and keep them under our control. Religion be gone, the state above all.

Source:

Fromm, Erich. 1962. *Beyond the Chains of Illusion: My Encounter with Marx and Freud.* New York: Bloomsbury.

Sigmund Freud

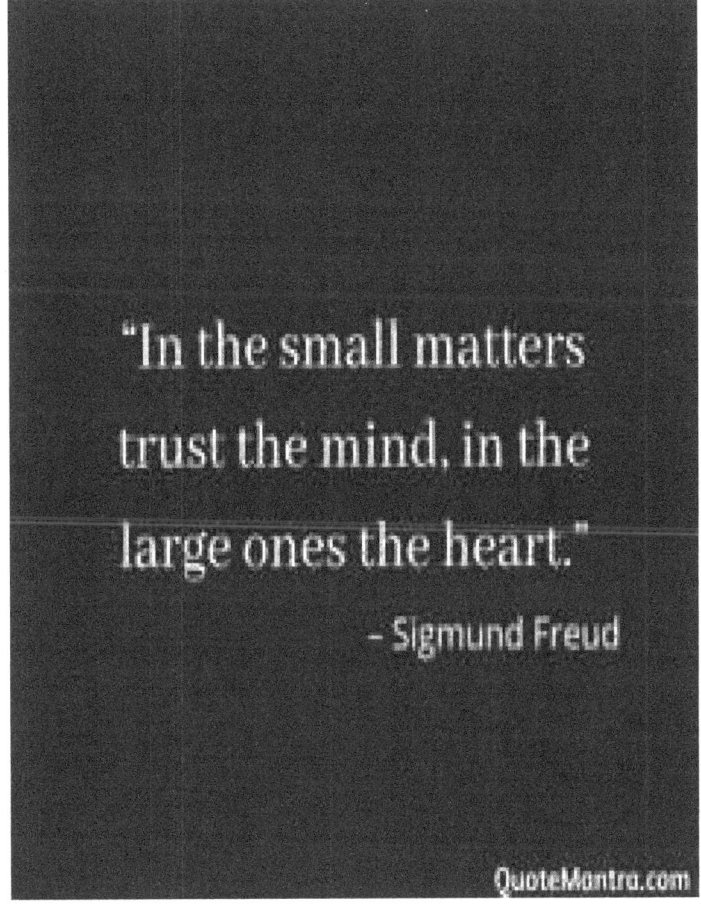

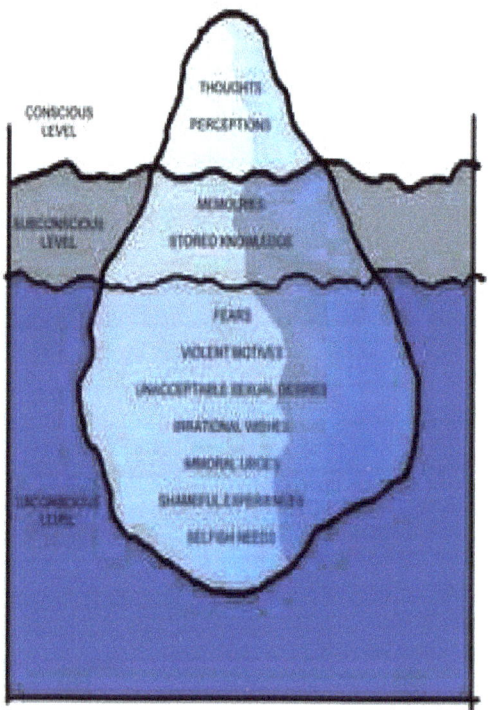

Chapter 20:

Neuroticism in America

Exodus 20: 3 "You shall have no other gods beside me."

1 Chronicle 16: 11 "Look to the Lord and his strength. Seek His face always."

Let's start from the beginning. No, not as in Genesis or Exodus above, but from one of the first authors I read in psychology that fascinated me, from the Freudian school of psychoanalysis, Karen Horney. [that's pronounced Horn-eye BTW] And so, this chapter may seem a little negative but it'll get better, trust me. One of her quotes that has remained with me until today, "The cry of the neurotic is 'woe unto you if you are not perfect'." Today we have a phenomenon called political correctness, progressing into 'wokeness'. It is a collective derangement, a phenomenon neurotic in nature pertaining to social and political thought that shouts at us - 'woe unto you if you are not perfect'. You have to be like us; you have to think like us. We are correct.

The 'Big Five Personality Test' is a current popularly used test by clinics and clinicians to determine personality traits. Summarized in the chart below, neuroticism is one of five traits that people carry with them to varying degrees.

The Big Five dimension traits

	Low Scorers	High Scorers
Extroversion	Loner, Quiet, Passive, Reserved	Joiner, Talkative, Active, Affectionate
Neuroticism	Calm, Even-tempered, Comfortable, Unemotional	Worried, Temperamental, Self-conscious, Emotional
Conscientiousness	Negligent, Lazy, Disorganized, Late	Conscientious, Hard-working, Well-organized, Punctual
Agreeableness	Suspicious, Critical, Ruthless, Irritable	Trusting, Lenient, Soft-hearted, Good-natured
Openness to experience	Down-to-earth, Uncreative, Conventional, Uncurious	Imaginative, Creative, Original, Curious

Pinterest

It recognizes neuroticism as a person's propensity toward anxiety and worry, depression and self-doubt, shame and guilt, deviance and envy. They generally experience a lot of stress, irritability and hostility. This series of negative, uncomfortable emotions permeates America and their personal solution is to get control. You must think like us. Kind of like 'body snatchers' from the movie *'Invasion of the Body Snatchers'*. But let's be clear. Neurosis is common, and in being a common trait among us, it is then normal in a sense. All of us exhibit neurotic traits to a certain degree. Psychosis, on the other hand, is not common, it is not normal, and psychotics cannot cope in this world. They are removed from reality. Family and friends were chatting one evening around the dinner table about the popular 1990s TV show 'Seinfeld. Who was your favorite character? Who did you like most? Unanimously it was Kramer. Of course, I said. Everyone likes Kramer. He's nuts. Our dinner guests each had his own problems with Elaine, Jerry, George, Newman. Of course, you don't like them. They are us - the neurotic, self-serving urban culture of America, regardless of city. It doesn't have to be Manhattan.

Anxiety and Worry

So how does Dr. Horney, a neo-Freudian, paint westerners; that is, citizens of our western culture? Ours is an anxiety ridden culture, yet so often people don't recognize it. They may deny its existence or cover it up. The cell phone culture, texting, gossiping, the computer life, are all elements of anxiety without recognizing it. Granted these elements of culture [computers and texting] did not exist in 1939, but anxiety did. It is just worse. Today they may more likely hide it in alcohol or drugs or a myriad of other distractions to relieve the discomfort. This may include involvement in non-essential activities to an excessive degree: sports, entertainment, gossip, sex, finances, money and career. Our other gods. And so, one thing is that neurotics seek affection to protect themselves from anxiety or in contrast may even be submissiveness toward others to help maintain an internal secure balance. Then there is the quest for power over others, manipulative types looking to protect themselves. Finally, they may withdraw and not contend with the world or cope with it one way or another. How's that? - watch an exorbitant amount of TV, hang on Facebook or Twitter, eat a midnight snack, order that extra Margarita, reclusively and overly love their stamp collection.

Depression and Self Doubt

This competitive culture sure takes its toll on people. Dr. Horney [1950] calls it the center of our neurotic conflicts. Competition in business, sports, career and professional ambition all foster comparative perceptions of each other. This excessive quest for power, prestige and possessions in our society especially is the focus of our competition. Did we match up with our foe, our neighbor, our cousin, our brother? It becomes a matter of winning or not winning, victory or failure. The outcome is a collective envy, resentment and hostility. The cultural landscape of winners and losers breeds feelings of inferiority and personal insignificance as common psychic disorders. People develop attitudes towards failure and success. Today we find a common approach to dress, or should I say dressing down. Brought down to a common level it is chic to have holes in our jeans, baggy pants and even worn below our butts. The well-dressed of yesteryear is frowned upon, the sign of success. Witness and major league baseball game of the 1950s and we'll see all the attendants dressed in suits and sporting hats. Strange today. Our individualist, competitive culture generates rivalry, hostility and fear between groups occupations and persons. It all effects our self-esteem.

Low self-esteem, our rampant negative self-evaluation, often comes about through both our social comparisons and comparing ourselves to our personal failures. We all fall short of the glory of God - the coulda, woulda, shoulda in our lives and even our shouldn't haves. Or in other words, our regrets that too often return to our minds. We are sorry for what we have done, what we have failed to do and what we should have done better. And so our self-confidence wanes, we build up negative self-talk and we look for security due to our fear of failure. Dr. Horney points out the emotional distress, anxieties, substance abuse and even depression from all our competitive striving. People will avoid it all, withdraw, seek the support of drugs or alcohol. Violence and abusive behavior spreads, anger and even suicide. It all is increasing as our culture deteriorates.

Guilt and Anger

Neurotic guilt feelings are a paramount characteristic in the culture. People end up blaming themselves for whatever reason concerning the issues permeating their lives. It is tough to cope. "Life is so awful, it is full of reality." Their inner self does not match their social self. What did I do wrong, why don't they like me? I'm a wonderful person. Is it me or others? Self-accusations have given way to the blame game of the media. White liberal guilt is current, as well as self-righteous anger imposed upon others. And so, whether one is guilty or not, the subconscious feeling of guilt is joined by an excessive defense against it. You can't tell them anything without a verbal and often times violent reaction. And they continue to blame others for not being their idealized self. Neurotics also fear disapproval. They want to be liked; they want to be loved. God forbid they annoy others, or disagree with an opinion. Guilt can also bring about aggression and hostility in the form of anger, envy and the desire to humiliate.

Alcoholism often is rooted in guilt and anger. They may drink to tell somebody off, to gain power over their foe. It can erupt into violence. But guilt and anger have its manifestations also in contempt, sarcasm, snobbishness, distrust, jealousy, or all of the above.

Deviance and Envy

Anne Henderschott [2002, 2020] has elaborated on the current politics of deviance and envy that exacerbates our personal tendencies toward anger. I call this institutionalized neuroticism. It gets its help from the administrative state and the democratic left. Promote deviance as opposed to the moral order. Eliminate the concept of deviance and eliminate guilt. Promote anger against the moral majority and its foundation, Christianity. Demoralize everybody and bring us all down to a lower level. What else can result but more neuroticism.

So in terms of deviance, to what are we referring? Well here is a list of modern decadent behaviors that some how are labeled as diseases, or normal not immoral behaviors. They eliminate personal responsibility.

1. Drug addiction and alcoholism;
2. Homelessness;
3. Mental illness;
4. Pedophilia;
5. Sexual orientations;
6. Promiscuity;
7. Suicide;

Here is one example. Closer to the 21st Century, Saint Pope John Paul II referred to the philosophy of the darling of the left Herbert Marcuse as 'the culture of death'. Marcuse tries to enlighten us on the inconvenience of the reality of death. We must be emancipated from the anxiety, worry and fear of death by more rationality and understanding of its meaning. Why allow our loved ones to die and at the same time experience such misery? Let us give them the opportunity to die at a time of their own choosing - ie. Euthanasia. That's the solution.

Anne Henderschott's *Politics of Envy* [2020] is a treatise of institutionalized neuroticism. Resentment of success, hatred of the rich, envy of the so called privileged is promoted so as to somehow enhance social justice. Further, competition and resentment of our successful friends can be the deadly sin fomenting neuroticism.

To create envy is to foment a movement toward equality or in today's terminology wokeness and equity. All are the same regardless of merit and only equity can be moral. Only the administrative state can make it that way. Christianity of course views it quite differently. To the Christian it is up to the individual and his relationship to God, his laws and his guidance. Relying on social and governmental structure has its latent dysfunctions. Summarily, let's say lack of freedom, more control, leftist ideological wokeness, and anti-Christianity at the least. It is all humanly unnatural; ie. Neuroticism.

Sources

Horney, Karen. 1937. *The Neurotic Personality of Our Time*. New York: W. W. Norton.

Horney, Karen. 1950. *Neuroses and Human Growth: The Struggle Toward Self-Realization*. New York: W. W. Norton.

Marcuse, Herbert. 1964. *One Dimensional Man*. Boston: Beacon.

Chapter 21:

Psychological Narcissism and the Administrative State

Galatians 2:20 "I have been crucified with Christ. It is no longer I who live, but Christ who lives in me. And the life I now live in the flesh I live by faith in the Son of God, who loved me and gave himself for me."

Luke 9:23 'And he said to all, "If anyone would come after me, let him deny himself and take up his cross daily and follow me."

Galatians 5:24 "And those who belong to Christ Jesus have crucified the flesh with its passions and desires."

Karen Horney [1950], the neo-Freudian and one of the first psychologists to explain to the public the nature of narcissism I still believe was spot on. Self-glorification, perfectionism and vindictiveness, common characteristics in western culture, sure gives a narcissist a lot to murmur about. I approached a gentleman in the foyer of our church one Sunday after mass. I wanted know if he was related to a fellow I knew with the same last name, and in the process tried to reach my hand out in order to befriend someone new. This gentleman was a great guy, so he told me. He proceeded to say well no, not related but continued on to tell me his life story and accomplishments. Not much really. He was dapper, dressed so nice and reminded me of one of the boys from the old neighborhood, Brooklyn. Watch out if you cross him or say something unappreciated in any way. I couldn't get a word in myself. An average person to most, he's narcissistic in the normal American way. While talking to my new friend [never talked to him again as he never even recognized me afterwards] he brought up his opinions of other ethnic groups [won't mention which] and how less than equal they were because of his perception of their values not meeting his standards. One of the best quotes I've always remembered of Dr. Horney for the neurotic, "Woe unto you if you are not perfect." He certainly was. Tough people to live with too.

No one has elaborated more on our narcissistic culture than Christopher Lasch [1979, xvi-xviii]. A Christian himself, he tried to live by the three scriptural quotes above. He saw it coming and here we are, a dying culture of competitiveness, individualism and decadence. Ours is a nation haunted by anxiety unable to face the future because of narcissistic self-absorption and aggrandizement. People live for themselves, not their ancestry or even their children. Egocentric, grandiose perceptions of self, lack of empathy toward others, these are the characteristics of the narcissist personality type. How that plays out in our culture is the main focus of Lasch's *The Culture of Narcissism*. It appears that bureaucracy is the solution.

Over 40 years later Lasch's view of the dependency on the state is ever more clear. And it is narcissism that gives way to this trend. [Lasch, 1979: 223- 239] Whether corporate or governmental, bureaucracy dominates our lives. It's a complicated world and large-scale organizations appear as most efficient in meeting the needs of society. And so bureaucracies grow and grow. A powerful method of social organization, bureaucracies strive to reach their goals and purposes and successful as they are, they thus take on a life of their own. Their intent is to expand; they just can't help themselves. As corporations grow, as government administration expands, these social configurations called into being rationalize their existence. They must continue, expand and fulfill a purpose. We are the sexual state, the welfare state, the technocratic state all there as a solution to our personal dysfunctions. The Democrat Party of the United States knows this all too perfectly. Whereas Presidents past have always warned us of balancing the budget, today's efforts led by the Democrat Party is entrenching us into more and more spending and debt, more and more organizational control, more and more bureaucracy from which we many never be able to extricate ourselves. Further, the purpose for the passing of new laws is to protect any of the new agendas. Sexual deviance is protected by new laws; new administrative agencies are protected by new laws; the cause for educational and racial reparation requires new agencies, more money and new laws; the propaganda of global warming requires new agencies, more money and legislation to protect it all. It is all on purpose. The administrative state's goals and fulfillment of its ideological agenda, control of the populace, control of corporate capitalism. Previously in history that was called socialism or communism. Today it is progressivism. Not all that efficient any longer, red tape results by the expansion of rules and regulations and procedures to confound us all. It is not to help the citizenry, it is to maintain power and control over the citizenry. People begin to feel more like automatons, objects more than than humans. People, both worker and client, feel estranged from all these rules, roles and functions of bureaucracy, alienated and undervalued. The human touch is lost. Add the increasing use of technology at home and office, and you've got the makings of body snatchers, zombie culture of intolerance of resisters to the system. Call on the corporate world and government to combine efforts and the totalitarian nature of the ideology is made clear. Even the difficulties in raising children brings on the bureaucracy of the public school system to control and overcome our parenting responsibilities. Offices, cubicles, organization of time, overly scheduled and procedural lives is the arrived at as the answer. Each organizational cell with its own rationality and ideology to guide it, in conjunction with the prevailing progressive overreaching ideology is the current mind set-in present-day society and government. It's the deep state.

The Democrat Party leads the field in bureaucratic organization and control. It is the secular form of maternalism and paternalism in helping build the new order. "It takes a village," says Hillary Clinton, as long as the village is the overreaching control of the federal bureaucracy. "I have been elected to unite the people of our country," says President Biden. Yes, as long as we all submit to the even more overreaching control of the federal bureaucracy and the ideology of the administrative state. Narcissism allowed it all because of its own lack of sense of responsibility. Let the government take care of it all since we've made a mess by ourselves. Let the new priests of secular psychology and sociology tell us what to think and solve our problems. They're professionals and bureaucrats at the same time. By our egocentricity, self-aggrandizement, and neurotic decadence, we abdicate our responsibility and become dependent. Cultural and moral authority are no longer in the hands of our churches and parents, but rather the administrative state and its ideologues, the media and college profs. We have become dependent on them and they want it that way.

Source:

Horney, Karen. 1950. *Neurosis and Human Growth: the Struggle Toward Self-Realization.* New York: W. W. Norton.

Lasch, Christopher. 1979. *The Culture of Narcissism: American Life in the Age of Diminishing Expectations.* New York: W.W. Norton.

For further discussion and research

Part VII - Freud

1. Who are the Neo-Freudians and how do they differ in their ideas on psychology and psychoanalysis from Sigmund Freud?

2. Appraise this author's contention of America as a neurotic and narcissistic state. Give support for your answer.

3. One of Freud's greatest contributions were his concepts of 'defense mechanisms' What were they and how did they function?

PART VIII:

Christianity and Socialism

Chapter 22:

Socialism from a Catholic's Perspective

After all the failures of socialism throughout world history, the so-called intelligentsia of the world have returned to it: the climate avengers, the government bureaucrats, the global resetters, the income redistributors, the woke corporate leaders. It hasn't been instituted right, and we'll do it right they say, on a global scale. And the U. S. has to join in. In believing so, the left has followed the leading socialist thinkers of the 18th, 19th and 20th centuries presented in this book. Break down our borders, destroy our culture, malign our heroes, attack our religions, tear apart our economic system, all promoted by the above philosophers. What they have left out of the equation is God, Christianity and to this author, Catholicism.

Let me be clear, Catholicism and socialism cannot co-exist. As much as apologists for socialism note the socialist and communal nature of the first Christians, they are wrong. As much as apologists for socialism cry out about the Christian nature of their ideology, and at the same time the socialist nature of Christianity, they are wrong. There is nothing wrong with sharing things in common in a community. Many small communities have experienced this throughout history. Translate that onto a centralized government for a nation of 200, 300 or 400 million, a nation of 1 - 1.5 billion, a world of 8 billion and it no longer resembles those Christian communities shortly after Jesus Christ walked this planet. The varied technological, industrial and political complexities, let alone cultural complexities preclude any such thing. Unless of course we have a centralized controlling power that imposes equity and equality upon all.

And there can be no stronger support for the ideas of capitalism than what would the Kingdom of Heaven be like as found in scripture -

Matthew 25: 14-28 -

14 "Again, it will be like a man going on a journey, who called his servants and entrusted his wealth to them. **15** To one he gave five bags of gold, to another two bags, and to another one bag, each according to his ability. Then he went on his journey. **16** The man who had received five bags of gold went at once and put his money to work and gained five bags more.

17 So also, the one with two bags of gold gained two more. **18** But the man who had received one bag went off, dug a hole in the ground and hid his master's money.

19 "After a long time the master of those servants returned and settled accounts with them. **20** The man who had received five bags of gold brought the other five. 'Master,' he said, 'you entrusted me with five bags of gold. See, I have gained five more.'

21 "His master replied, 'Well done, good and faithful servant! You have been faithful with a few things; I will put you in charge of many things. Come and share your master's happiness!'

22 "The man with two bags of gold also came. 'Master,' he said, 'you entrusted me with two bags of gold; see, I have gained two more.'

23 "His master replied, 'Well done, good and faithful servant! You have been faithful with a few things; I will put you in charge of many things. Come and share your master's happiness!'

24 "Then the man who had received one bag of gold came. 'Master,' he said, 'I knew that you are a hard man, harvesting where you have not sown and gathering where you have not scattered seed. **25** So I was afraid and went out and hid your gold in the ground. See, here is what belongs to you.'

26 "His master replied, 'You wicked, lazy servant! So, you knew that I harvest where I have not sown and gather where I have not scattered seed? **27** Well then, you should have put my money on deposit with the bankers, so that when I returned, I would have received it back with interest.

28 "'So take the bag of gold from him and give it to the one who has ten bags. **29** For whoever has will be given more, and they will have an abundance. Whoever does not have, even what they have will be taken from them.

30 And throw that worthless servant outside, into the darkness, where there will be weeping and gnashing of teeth.'

Prime Minister Winston Churchill said it, "Socialism is a philosophical failure, the creed of ignorance, and the gospel of envy. It is where virtue is the equal sharing of misery."

The goal of socialism is communism, an atheistic, godless state of a government forced equality. It becomes a place where individual liberties are removed and replaced by state control. Private property is replaced by redistributing income toward the equity they demand. More threatening to our culture, it opposes the nuclear family, undermining it through the school as a substitute of parental authority. It opposes families by imposing a curriculum in direct opposition to Christian beliefs such as the current gender ideology. Socialism takes a materialist view on history and society promoting atheism and rejecting spirituality. Clearly even riot prone organizations like Black Lives Matter have openly admitted its intent on destroying the family, Christianity and divisions according to race. BLM, the unsuspecting followers of Marx and the father of communism, don't even realize Marx's own prejudices in his personal life toward nonwhite Europeans and mixing of the races. Socialism is the big lie.

No, socialism opposes private property and decentralization of power. It divides people through its historical approach of class warfare to give central government its opening toward control, and it opposes all religion, especially Catholicism. Catholicism is about worshiping and following Jesus Christ, Lord and Savior. It is a relationship with Jesus first and foremost - the way, the truth, and the life. Socialism can have no other Gods before it.

So what do we do about it? Isn't it funny? Every person from Cuba, every person from Eastern Europe, every person from Vietnam, everyone from Taiwan and Hong Kong who finds themselves in the United States today know what is going on. When they talk to Americans who were here before them, these Americans do not listen. That's not what's going on, they reply. They can't see it. And I repeat, Communism 21st century style is the current revolution led by intellectuals, technocrats, bureaucrats and the media. Not like in Russia, China, Cuba, Vietnam, Cambodia, but a lot more sophisticated. Tough enemy.

As proclaimed above, Catholicism disapproves of socialism in the strictest terms. Traditionally the church has dealt with politics in a number of ways and is not about to change course. Summarily, the church looks to cooperate with the government [obeying laws], challenge the government when necessary [opposing oppressive, immoral laws], compete with the government [hospital care, education, feeding the poor, housing the homeless] and go beyond the government by proclaiming the gospel. Sometimes the church has to separate from government in order to protect religious freedom [separation of church and state]. Never before has this been needed enough. So, being that the church consists of its members, they are required to participate in government, vote, defend their country, pay taxes and promote peace. Can we say this for the two arms of the democratic party - BLM and Antifa?

All our participation is needed especially due to the politicization of all institutions in America, a socialist and totalitarian tactic from the start. They politicize everything to pass on their ideological religion as the ubiquitous mind set required for all. Everything is political: sport, art, schools, curriculum, health care, corporate policy, even family and religion all infused with leftist ideology. No others allowed. Why even the Superbowl advertisement concerning Jesus and his concern for us was called fascist by AOC, Alexandria Ocasio-Cortez. Church attendance was restricted by state governments during the Covid 19 pandemic, and feminists condemn Catholic practice as male paternalism as if we are not allowed to follow our own religion. Everything is from a leftist ideological perspective.

On a personal level, I have found the answer through the writing of two gentlemen regarding the resistance toward this totalitarian march: Noble Prize Winner Alexandr Solzhenitsyn [2002], and Rod Dreher [2020] in his book *Live Not by Lies*. They both call to:

1. Live apart from the crowd in order to live in truth and not to get caught up in the left's group think propaganda, all the time fighting for free speech.

2. Remember our history and the history of totalitarian societies.

3. Cling to our families as resistance cells to totalitarianism, the place where we learn to love and live in truth.

4. Hold on to our religious beliefs, principles, faith and communities, the bedrock of resistance.

5. And finally in the words of Saint Padre Pio, continue to "Pray, hope and don't worry."

Source:

Black, Amy. 2008. *Beyond Left and Right*. Grand Rapids: Baker Books.

Dreher. Rod. 2020. *Live Not by Lies: A Manual for Christian Dissidents.* New York: Sentinel.

Solzhenitsyn, Alexandr. 2002. *The Gulag Archipelago Abridged.* New York: Harper Perennial.

Chapter 23:

Only Mass Enrollment in Christian Schools Can Save this Country

The Catholic school enrollment of the Archdiocese of Boston is close to 30% of the public-school enrollment. The central administration numbers are .05% of Catholic vs. Public schools. Public schools sure looks top heavy with regard to administrative costs. Granted, Catholic schools do not have departments of special education, vocational, and free lunches and breakfasts, nor the extensive transportation costs. They just focus their education on its children through a curriculum of God and country with as minimal a cost as possible. They focus on teacher commitment along with student achievement without the bureaucratic nature of its system. Catholic schools are both faith based and community oriented with a considerably higher level of achievement among its students with a higher level of high school completion and enrollment into college. In addition, students from lower income families achieve at a higher level than their public-school counter parts. Graduates tend to vote at a higher rate, earn higher salaries, and are more committed to community service as adults. Catholic schools work and at a cost much below public school. [Catholic World Mission, 2019]

Not only do Catholic schools work, they work better in urban areas and inner-city urban communities than their counter part public schools. The classroom discipline is better, the expectations are higher and the results follow. Parents are encouraged to get involved and their children receive a moral education besides higher level academics. There are many non-Catholics enrolled in Catholic schools, yet moral education is the first thing inculcated, not Catholicism itself.

As Bill Donahue points out in *Common Sense Catholicism: How to Resolve Our Cultural Crisis* [2019], Catholic schools excel in educational success through what is referred to as impulse control. That means character development and keeping impulses in check. This is accomplished through challenging work, a lot of homework, self-discipline and the 10 commandments. God permeates the curriculum, unheard of in public schools. Being answerable to God brings on self-restraint in an individual. Religion positively influences behavior in children. So, to paraphrase Pope Benedict XVI, it is a rounded education for the whole person.

Faculty and administrative support for its students is a primary determinant of student success in Catholic schools. With many inner-city children coming from broken families, this support is the key to success in that families are recognized as the number one variable for academic accomplishment. And family support is the ultimate factor for student success in any school system. Compare a Catholic high school to a public high school in structure, class size and support. In a public high school of 2000, 3000 or 4000 students, a child will attend school for four years and never once speak to an adult. He or she is lost in a sea of anonymity forced to cling to available support groups, cliques, gangs, crime, deviancy of all kinds. Who knows what devices might be available for such children. Probably the most pressing problem in America is the relation of its teenagers to adults. It is almost non-existent for many, and a healthier connection to society is lost.

Catholic high schools on the other hand, are rarely above 1000 - 1200 and generally in the hundreds. Class sizes are smaller, standards maintained and with-it moral education. No one is lost.

In sum, Catholic school enrollment results in higher graduation rates, and higher percentages of college admittance through curriculum and preparation. They have lower student teacher ratios, a strong sense of community and above all, learning moral values for Catholics and non-Catholics alike.

A former Catholic high school teacher myself, the most recent example of my experience with Catholic schools is our thrice yearly Knights of Columbus visits to Hope Rural School in Indiantown, FL. [Baglino, 2022] To this author, this small Catholic school, PK3 - 5 lives up to its name in giving hope to 140 children and to a nation of 330 million. How's that? You have to meet the kids. Hope Rural School provides a Catholic education that nurtures the Gospel values of mercy, justice and love. And that is just what you see when you arrive. A student population of such gentility, respect and love just gushes out toward visitors. It is the molding of Catholic character engendered to each from its curriculum and staff. Indiantown is a community of immigrant farm workers from Haiti, Mexico and Guatemala who have called this area home for decades. Holy Cross Catholic Church, Indiantown's only Catholic church is adjacent to the school campus and serves the community of just below 7,000. Demographics indicate a city of approximately 16% white, 12% black and 70% Hispanic. The school population is predominantly children of migrant farm workers with one student identifying himself as white and American. Speaking with the children is a joy. They speak of their tribulations through both the desert areas and rainy areas of Mexico to get here. They speak of the animals at night and fear they engender upon the migrants. They speak of the bandits at night and the fear further engendered. They speak of the illnesses endured throughout their ordeal. They speak of the hope they all had to get to

America and for their families to make a better life for themselves. They speak clearly about it because the major portion of the curriculum is the training of English writing, reading and speaking skills along with American history and culture. They are America's future. Success abounds over the past 40 years with graduates becoming, nurses, teacher, lawyers. If America is to return to sanity and morality it's through the education of our youth as witnessed in Catholic schools such as Hope Rural School and the 7,500 Catholic elementary and high schools through out the country. America is going through a period of what is called a 'collective mental derangement'. Push for state run school choice voucher systems in America to save us from this Marxist madness.

Source:

Baglino, Michael J. 2022. *What is So Special About Hope Rural School?* Catholic 365.com

https://catholicworldmission.org/catholic-education/2019.

Donahue, Bill. 2019. *Common Sense Catholicism: How to Resolve Our Cultural Crisis*. San Francisco: Ignatius.

Researched Case for Catholic Schools. 2020. Notre Dame University. Alliance for Catholic Education.

Chapter 24:

4 Characteristics Needed for Christian Leadership: The Future

One of the main themes of Christian author Alexandre Harvard is the development of leadership. Specifically, he states that his mission is to "Ignite hearts for greatness and transform the resultant fire into a powerful habit of the mind and the will." [Harvard, 2019] And that greatness in an individual cannot be realized without the essence of leadership: magnanimity and humility. That is, they have to challenge themselves to strive for greatness and at the same time serve others. Magnanimity and humility cannot be achieved however, without these 4 personal characteristics: prudence, courage, self-mastery, justice. Match these characteristics with your personal mission.

1. **Prudence** - A prudent man is sensible and discerning; thus, confident in decision making. He is knowledgeable while at the same time would not flaunt. Similarly, how could a flaunting person serve others? Prudence requires humility in order to serve.

John 16:13 "When the Spirit of truth comes, he will guide you into all the truth, for he will not speak on his own authority, but whatever he hears he will speak, and he will declare to you the things that are to come."

2. **Courage** - Have the daring to take risks, and yet with stick-to-itiveness? As endurance builds, fear diminishes and stability increases.

2 Timothy 1:7 "For God gave us a spirit not of fear but of power and love, and self-control."
1 Corinthians 16:13 "Be watchful, stand firm in the faith, act like men, be strong."

3. **Self-Mastery** - Everything in moderation and elimination of excessive indulgence is a requisite for self-mastery. Channel your energy to the mission at hand. Spirit and energy dominate over emotions and passions, power and pleasures.

Ephesians 5:18 "And do not get drunk with wine, for that is debauchery, but be filled with the Spirit."

4. **Justice** - Keeping it legal and equitable, is to be sure all get what they deserve or are entitled [but not in the political sense of today's progressive culture]. Without fairness let's say, the desire to serve is squelched.

Isaiah 1:17 "Learn to do good; seek justice, correct oppression; bring justice to the fatherless, plead the widow's cause."

So whatever talents you have, whatever mission you decide, your effectiveness will depend upon personal characteristics and its moral foundations. I sure hope Alexander Harvard has helped ignite your will and hearts as he has mine. See below for two of his motivating works. And let us look at Ron DeSantis.

Sources:

Harvard, Alexandre. 2019. *Created for Greatness*. New York: Scepter

Harvard, Alexandre. 2018. *From Temperament to Character: On Becoming a Virtuous Leader*. New York: Scepter

Chapter 25:

What is Servant Leadership?

Though not an endorsement of Governor Ron Desantis as President, allow me to use some examples of his leadership and style to explain what is needed in dealing with our current social and political dilemma. Recent TV political advertisements presented the case for re-electing Florida Governor Ron Desantis. One such ad included a former U. S. Naval officer referring to Ron Desantis as a 'true servant leader'. Such an impressive, honorable comment and admirable qualities spoken from one of his fellow Naval officers, it prompted me to seek out the characteristics of a 'true servant leader'.

Previous to serving as Governor of Florida, Ron Desantis graduated from Yale University and Harvard Law School. What strikes this author was his being captain of the Yale University Baseball Team. To me, always important - a regular guy. He was a Lieutenant in the U. S. Navy, deployed to Iraq and advisor to Seal Team One. He earned the Bronze Star,

Navy and Marine Corps Commendation Medal, Global War on Terrorism Service Medal and Iraq Campaign Medal. He subsequently won election to Florida's 6th congressional district as congressman before being elected Governor. That's it in a nutshell. And, he and his family are practicing Roman Catholics.

Is he a servant leader? Does he have a vision of the future for Floridians? Can he inspire and lead its citizens? Do we know his core values through his communication and actions? Is he for us and is it about us? [Perkins, 2000]

Proverbs 29: 18 "Where there is no vision, the people perish; but he that keepeth the law, happy is he."

First test for a political leader is preparedness and as Hurricane Ian approaches [at the time of this writing], it is being done. He made sure of it for each storm that has approached Florida since 2018. From there our Governor initiated such policies as election reform, and entrepreneurial education and training showing his preference toward economic leadership and a free market as opposed to command economies. He instituted executive actions against threats posed by China, Cuba, Iran, Russia, North Korea, Syria, Venezuela. These actions helped thwart cyber threats and real estate investments based on sceptical motives. He appointed trustees throughout our state university system assuring higher educational integrity in terms of finance and propaganda. Recently the governor has stymied the left's poisonous public school curriculum agenda of gender theory and critical race theory. Desantis has made known his recognition of our principles and rights under seige by the left. And so he eliminated the Florida state university and college policies of 'diversity , equity and inclusion' as antithetical to democracy and American values. Further he banned sex change procedure as health care procedures while at the same time signed the strongest pro-life bill in Florida history.

In the 1970s your humble author was a teacher of a required course in Florida public schools entitled 'Americanism vs. Communism'. This was while at the Hialeah Adult Education Center. The statewide text book used for this course was *Today's Isms,* helping create and awareness of the domestic and international forces working in this world, some for and some against the United States. Democrat governors discontinued the requirement, but Governor Desantis reinstituted a similar requirement.

Second, he's not a passive politician and it is not just words. BLM and Antifa riots are not tolerated in Florida, sanctuary cities banned and Chinese Communist land grabs in its rural sector were opposed. Ahead of the game, Governor Desantis has made it known from the start that he favors freedom over control, especially government control, both personally and economically. He kept the schools open, the churches open, the businesses open, and the masks off. He maintains that our schools teach values in keeping with western democratic values and traditional Christian/Judeo values. Of course the left starts calling names after successes like this. They have no argument. It is the governor of California who is the 'neo-fascist'. Theirs is a state of government control. Centralized control is the purpose of the left. Decentralization of power is their enemy. Opposition to the overturning of Roe vs. Wade is imperative for them, not only because of the abortion issue but because it brings these decisions out of the hands of the central government. This to the left is the solution to all problems as they see it. Fear of freedom and control is their motivation.

Proverbs 11: 3 "The integrity of the upright shall guide them: but the perverseness of transgressors shall destroy them."

On a personal level, Governor DeSantis is a stickler for personal integrity. He sends illegals to Massachusetts, Washington, D. C. and New York because he knows Pres. Biden and these urban mayors are not. He confronts them for they lean on federal policy and leftist political ideology, not themselves. It is called hypocrisy; their personal lives do not live their ideological beliefs.

Isaiah 41: 10 "Fear not, for I am with you; be not dismayed, for I am your God; I will strengthen you, I will help you, I will uphold you with my righteous right hand."

This is the leader attempting us back on track toward our rightful future. He is one of us too. He gets his strength from God, not Karl Marx. Recently before this writing, Desantis won the gubernatorial race by 20 points, a landslide. Why? Because Desantis won by his example and the citizens of Florida love him. He has an awareness of that existential reality opposing political parties intend for this country. Servant leaders are grounded in reality. Hard work and willingness to sacrifice is his style. He's a fighter. Not sure he would make a good president yet, but as a state governor, we see the results.

Source:

Perkins, Bill. 2000. *Awaken the Leader Within: How the Wisdom of Jesus can Unleash Your Potential.* Grand Rapids, Michigan: Zondervan Publishing House.

Chapter 26

The Ongoing Prejudices: Anti-Catholicism and Anti Semitism

Part A Anti-Catholicism

Are these cultural, psychological or political prejudices? You're right, all three. I'll try to focus on current trends rather than historical foundations, but not entirely. Anti Semitism is the history of the world. Anti-Jewish prejudice has existed for 5,000 years. A slave culture led by God and Moses into the promise land, prejudice against Judaism continues today. Jesus, the King of the Jews and the fulfillment of the Torah, founded the Catholic Church after the Jewish first 3,000+ years. So, in this regard we can see the connection of the Judeo-Christian tradition leading to 2023. And since the current movement against our Western civilization and its Judeo-Christian foundation grows, it is no wonder that Catholicism receives its more than fair share of prejudice.

Up front, the voice of anti-Catholic prejudice in America is none other than the Democrat Party. If any Democrat politician calls himself Catholic, it is a form of Catholicism unbeknownst to the Magisterium of the church. Let's take Joe Biden. He supports and even promotes abortion, he supports and promotes euthanasia, he supports and promotes gay marriage, he supports and promotes the LGBTQ movement, he supports and promotes transgenderism, he supports and promotes radical secular feminism, he supports and promotes the globalist political agenda. Democrat politicians call Catholics extremist because they do not support their anti-Christian agendas. All of a sudden, their new agendas are normal and 2,000 years of Christian history which helped form western civilization and its successes are declared abnormal.

Your humble author is a member of the Catholic Knights of Columbus. Vice President Harris as the radical feminist she is, decried and denounced our group because it is a group of all men. Little does she know that our church has women's groups too. Little does she know that we have men and women's groups together. Little does she know that we as a group of Christian men help feed and clothe the poor, visit the incarcerated, give aid to the sick, give financial support to education, help our veterans, help our disabled, give aid and shelter to the homeless, and a myriad of other services to meet the needs of peoples all over the world. We do this with our time and money, not someone else's money as Vice President Harris wants to do. She has no regard for the nature of our church, nor respect for our religion. Rather, it has to change and conform to liberal ideology. Then and only then will it accept Catholicism. Joe Biden fits the bill. Supreme court nominees are accused of being out of the mainstream where their Catholic dogma shouts out to the public. Such is the accusation of California Senator Feinstein. But let us depart from political prejudices.

The TV and Movie industry loves to portray Catholicism in a less than positive light. [Donahue, 2018: 259] *Dogma, The DaVinci Code,* and *The Name of the Rose* are a few films that come to mind. The inquisition is always brought up both on screen and in college classrooms with all of its false accusations and disinformation. Some of my previous college students would claim [while not realizing I was Catholic] that they would force Catholic hospitals to perform abortions. Immoralities, as in the recent child abuse scandals accuse Catholicism, not the homosexual priests who do not practice their religion and never should have been allowed priesthood status in the first place. Even though there are so many liberals who support NAMBLA, The North American Man/Boy Love Association and its practices. Plus, there are just as many cases in other churches synagogues, and public schools. Imprisoning prolife activists who have not broken any law is the latest in government harassment of Catholics.

Anti Catholic murmurs abound from its false images to its unchanging theology. God's laws remain, forever and ever. Nothing you can do about it. As one TV preacher once expressed, when Jesus returns, liberals around the world will send up their missiles against him shouting, "go home, we don't want you here, this is our planet!"

Part B Anti Semitism

Now for the psychology of anti-antisemitism. It's classic in the nature of prejudice. It pertains to stereotypes, scapegoats, social mobility, social change and the religion itself.

Stereotyping is an exaggerated belief about a certain group of people. It is a mental process which helps serve to reject that group - racial, ethnic, religious. Murmuring over stereotypical views of Jews as more intelligent renders a subconscious jealousy and resentment. Accusations of shrewdness and clannishness foments an easier focus for blame. Especially in times of economic turmoil, Jews are blamed for their control of the economy, the media, the banks, the retail industry, the entertainment industry. They'll say money is their God. Their tendency to keep apart and exclude gentiles, builds resentment further. These are exaggerated perceptions. Subscribing to such stereotypes that all ethnic groups carry with them to one degree or another, justifies their dislike toward Jews. As to their abilities with money and the economy, well Jews are an urban people and have a lot of experience with matters of finance and economics. They are better at it than the rest of us, though that has changed. You don't have to be Jewish. Got lots of rich non-Jewish friends. One sociological study pointed out Episcopalians as the richest religious group.

Singling out people for unmerited blame and justified negative treatment is scapegoating. Persecute and blame the outsiders and minorities when things go bad. Blame those of urban success though we have not been so urbanized as of yet. Some stereotypes have some bit of truth to them. A friend from Minneapolis stands out in this regard. He hates what calls the local 'yuppies'. He lives on welfare and a migrant from the rural south. These so called yuppies are trained in many fields, and they worked for college degrees They commit themselves toward more achievement and accomplishment in their professions and climbing that corporate ladder of success. They live in Edina and St. Louis Park, two Minneapolis suburbs with a high Jewish population. It's their fault and he blames them for his failures and calls them racist. Which brings us to the sociological phenomena of social mobility.

The above mentioned yuppies have as a group shifted their social status in an upward direction.

Social Mobility refers moving up or down the social strata in terms of wealth, education, associations, neighborhood location. Social status can be either achieved or ascribed. People are free to achieve for themselves the personal advancement aspired to. People are also born into that level through generational location, religion, race, family acquired wealth. Studies show that Jews seem to take on more prejudice when there is a falling off occupational ladders of success by other groups. [Allport, 1954: 224] Combine this with social change and we have a perfect storm toward anti antisemitism. During the Russian Revolution it was Jews who got the heat for being capitalist. During leftist political upheavals it was the Jews who got the heat for being communist. Can't win. The interplay of social change, social mobility, stereotyping and scapegoating all lead to anti antisemitism. My Sicilian immigrant grandfather used to curse Jews every time he was frustrated about something. I guess he thought it was their fault. I couldn't understand why he murmured so.

Aside from their experiences in Egypt, religious persecution can be traced to Roman times. Though Christians were more persecuted than Jews during the Roman Empire era, Jews were rejected since they held so fast to worshiping their God and not the gods of the Roman empire. And they would not share their God but kept within their own culture since they considered themselves chosen. God was for them. That annoyed the Romans. So they were talked about, avoided, discriminated against, physically attacked and 2,000 years later almost exterminated. [Allport, 1954: 14]

As to the state of Israel, surprisingly Marxists have a mixed view. Anti-religious Marcuse supported Israel on identy and geopolitical grounds. Conservatively religious Erich Fromm, contemporary of Marcuse and also of German Jewish Marxist origins opposed the state of Israel on anti-biblical grounds. To other religious groups [Protestant, Catholic, Muslim, Hindu] views of the Israeli state are also diverse. Therefore, opposition to support for Israel as being antisemitic is debatable. But to these religions, Judaism itself is in error, and vice versa. No one belief system seems to have united the world and an apparently competitive existence has developed into strife. With regard to Christians, Jews were blamed for the persecution and crucifixion of Christ. Jews accuse Christ of His audaciousness for claiming to be the Son of God. And the pursuance and connection of power, prestige and wealth with religion foments the hostilities engendered in any society. People like to connect power, prestige and wealth with religion from many a standpoint, back and forth. Secular liberalism is yet another religion guilty of it all. Strongly antisemitic and anti-Catholic, it seeks to control universally via the new world order. We owe our allegiance to God first, not the state. We all become guilty in our beliefs and perceptions, religious or secular. Striving for truth at the end is all that matters.

Source:

Allport, Gordon W. 1954. *The Nature of Prejudice*. New York: Addison - Wesley.

Donahue, Bill. 2019. *Common Sense Catholicism*. San Francisco: Ignatius Press.

Chapter 27:

SUMMARY and CONCLUSION

Break down the culture. Attack Christianity. Disparage the cultural heroes of capitalism. Gramsci in a nutshell. Infuse sociological conflict theory into the curriculum and speak for the oppressed and disenfranchised. Raise Marxist consciousness among the intelligentsia and privileged too. Be intolerant to their position. So said Marcuse. To Hegel it was necessary to offer alternatives to the God concept, to foster the state as the highest authority. Rights and freedoms came from the state, not God. We are as God. God is nothing more than our projection. Rely on the material world of our making to make it better. Feuerbach's materialist view of society believed media persuasion and propaganda would help bring progress along. The history of the world is the history of class struggle between the working class and the capitalist ruling class. Marx called for workers of the world to unite in a violent revolution if necessary. Socialism would then lead to communism.

Darwin's research led to his theory of evolution claiming natural selection and survival of the fittest. Social Darwinism claimed superiority of certain groups over others and society divided by superior and inferior groups of race, ethnicity and gender. This existed within nations and colonial powers. Sexual and moral rebellion took a giant leap forward as Sigmund Freud came on to the scene in Europe and the United States. Gramsci and Marcuse pounced on it.

Here are the seven philosophers, not liberating but autocratic and authoritarian in nature. The Democrat Party of the United States is clearly a left leaning organization, many are socialists, many are communists, many are useful idiots for the cause as Lenin referred liberals. Sex, race and climate change are their issues. But they are not the agenda. The agenda is a socialist revolution to change America as President Obama called. They don't care about the climate, the poor or gender issues. These issues are exploited for their true agenda, breaking down our capitalist economic system toward global socialism with America joining in.

Professional revolutionaries are funded by corporate elites to organize rebellion in order to disrupt society and spread their propaganda. The unsuspecting fall for it. The words sound nice but the so-called liberals have no concern for the their constituents nor the issues they promote: gender, race, poor, climate. Through it all Christianity has a battle on its hands. Only recently have Christians caught on to what is transpiring. A Bishop in California was just murdered, socially conscious Catholic students are attacked and falsely accused because they wore MAGA hats. Politicians begin to have religious requirements for Supreme Court Justice positions. Major League baseball teams promote the LGBTQ agenda while attacking Christianity. However, these politicians and corporate elites turn their backs when college students illegally march and demonstrate at their homes. And it is the Trump derangement syndrome and abortion mania that defines them. They have to have it their way since their ideology tells them socialism is inevitable, deterministic and authoritarianism is their ideology's nature.

The intelligentsia has no qualms in collaborating with the enemy, and with falsely accusing our own leaders. They of course are more enlightened and the ends justifies the means. They confer with Cuban and Venezuelan leaders, Chinese operatives, Russian dignitaries. It's all for the high-minded intent on international cooperation at America's expense.

Is there a way out of all of this? We are so outnumbered and the power centers of the world have their plans to enact. Rod Dreher has these suggestions:

1. Live apart from the crowd in order to live in truth and not to get caught up in the left's group think propaganda, all the time fighting for free speech. Farenheit 451.

2. Remember our history and the history of totalitarian societies. Alexandr Solzhenytsin.

3. Cling to our families as resistance cells to totalitarianism, the place where we learn to love and live in truth. Western and Christian heritage.

4. Hold on to our religious beliefs, principles, faith and communities, the bedrock of resistance. Judaeo-Christianity.

5. Support our Christian leaders.

Michael J. Baglino has these suggestions: pray, go to church, hold on to your families, send your children to Catholic schools.

This author is no way what the left might suggest - a right winger, but in Marxist dogma, all opponents must be classified on the right. Everyone must be their enemy if they don't agree. I just see the events unfolding and its secular founding philosophers wishing they were alive today. I see it from a Christian perspective, not right or left but straight up to God, and the Body of Christ will persevere and reign. That's inevitable too.

For discussion and research

Part VIII - Christianity and Socialism

1. Conceive a curriculum that would be effective in reestablishing western education and values in our schools and society.

2. Assess which of today's politicians and leaders you can identify as servant leaders.

References:

Allport, Gordon. 1954. *The Nature of Prejudice.* New York: Addison Wesley.

Antell, Gerson and Walter Harris. 2005. *Economic Institutions and Analysis, 4th ed.* New York: Amsco Publications.

Baglino, Michael J. 2023. *Florida Meets Europe.* New York: LT Publishers.

Baglino, Michael J. 2022. "5 Anti Christian Philosophers Who Ruined America. www.Catholic365.com

Baglino, Michael J. 2023. Just What is Marxism Anyway? *Europe Meets Florida.* New York: LT Publishing.

Baglino, Michael. 1992. *Relevance of the Community College Curriculum to the InternationalStudent.* digitalcommons.fiu.edu/etd/1368/"

Baglino, Michael J. "What Might Marxist University Professors be Responsible For?" *More From a Florida Catholic.* San Francisco: The Penguin Writers.

Baglino, Michael J. 2022. "What is So Special About Hope Rural School in Indiantown, FL?" *Catholic 365.com*

Black, Amy. 2008. *Beyond Left and Right.* Grand Rapids: Baker Books.

https://catholicworldmission.org/catholic-education/2019.

Compendium Catechism of the Catholic Church. 2017. Rome: Libreria Editrice Vaticana.

DeBakcsy, Dale. 2014. Ludwig Feuerbach. *Philosophy Now.*

Donahue, Bill. 2019. *Common Sense Catholicism: How to Resolve Our Cultural Crisis.* San Francisco: Ignatius.

Dreher. Rod. 2020. *Live Not by Lies: A Manual for Christian Dissidents.* New York: Sentinel.

Farr, Arnold. 2012. "Herbert Marcuse" *The Stanford Encyclopedia of Philosophy.* Edward N. Zalta.

"Fighting Critical Theory." October, 2021. *CatholicVote.Org.*

Fromm, Erich. 1962. *Beyond the Chains of Illusion: My Encounter with Marx and Freud.* New York: Bloomsbury.

Gramsci, Antonio and David Forgacs [Ed.] 2001. *The Antonio Gramsci Reader: Selected Writings 1916 - 1935.* New York University Press.

Harvard, Alexandre. 2019. *Created for Greatness.* New York: Scepter

Harvard, Alexandre. 2018. *From Temperament to Character: On Becoming a Virtuous Leader*. New York: Scepter

Harvey, Van, 2011. "Ludwig Andreas Feuerbach", *The Stanford Encyclopedia of Philosophy*. Edward N. Zalta (ed.)

Hegel View on State and Civil Society. "Why Hegel Knew There Would be Days Like These." Article1000.com

Henderschott, Anne. 2002. *The Politics of Deviance*. San Francisco: Encounter Books.

Henderschott, Anne. 2020. *The Politics of Envy*. Manchester, NH: Crisis Publications.

Holy Bible, ESV. 2001. Wheaton, IL.: Crossway.

Horney, Karen. 1937. *The Neurotic Personality of Our Time*. New York: W. W. Norton.

Horney, Karen. 1950. *Neuroses and Human Growth: The Struggle Toward Self-Realization*. New York: W. W. Norton.

Krason, Stephen A. 2022. *The Left vs. Realities of Race in America*. The Catholic Social Science Review. Vol. 27. The Society of Catholic Social Scientists.

Krason, Stephen A. 2022. *Needed Now: An Organized Effort and Plan to Defeat the Left*. The

Catholic Social Science Review. Vol 27. The Society of Catholic Social Scientists.

Krason, Stephen A. 2022. "What the Democratic Party has Become." *The Catholic Social Science Review*. Vol. 27. The Society of Catholic Social Scientists.

Lasch, Christopher. 1979. *The Culture of Narcissism: American Life in the Age of Diminishing Expectations*. New York: W.W. Norton.

McNamara, Robert. 2021. "Biography of Charles Darwin: Originator of the Theory of Evolution." *www.Thoughtco.com*

Marcuse, Herbert. 1968. *One Dimensional Man*. Boston: Beacon Press.

Marcuse, Herbert. 1965. "Repressive Tolerance" *A Critique of Pure Tolerance*. Boston: Beacon Press.

Martin, James. 2023. "Antonio Gramsci", *The Stanford Encyclopedia of Philosophy*. Edward N. Zalta and Uri Nodelman [eds.]

Morse, Jennifer Roback. 2018. The Sexual State: How Elite Ideologies are Destroying Lives and Why the Church Was Right All Along. Charlotte, NC. Tan Books.

New American Bible. 2011. Washington, D. C. : World Catholic Press.

Parsons, Talcott et. al. Editor. 1961. *Theories of Society*. New York: The Free Press.

Perkins, Bill. 2000. *Awaken the Leader Within: How the Wisdom of Jesus can Unleash Your Potential.* Grand Rapids, Michigan: Zondervan Publishing House.

Prager, Dennis. 2017. *Leftism is not Liberalism.* Townhall.

Rectenwald, Michael. Dec. 2021. "What is the Great Reset?" *Imprimus.*

Redding, Paul, 2020."Georg Wilhelm Friedrich Hegel", *The Stanford Encyclopedia of Philosophy.* Edward N. Zalta (ed.)

Researched Case for Catholic Schools. 2020. Notre Dame University. Alliance for Catholic Education.

Rodriguez, Peter. 2010. *Why Economies Rise or Fall.* The Great Courses.

Rogers, Adrian. "Five Anti Christian Philosophers Who Ruined America." Palm City, FL: WCNO Radio.

Solzhenitsyn, Alexandr. 2002. *Gulag Archipelago: Abridged. New York:* Harper and Row.

Thiroux, Jacques P. and Keith W. Krasemann. 2009.
Ethics: Theory and Practice. Upper Saddle River, N. J.: Prentice Hall

World Bank Open Data: *World Development Indicators, 2020*

BIO -

Dr. Michael J. Baglino, Ed. D. is a retired college teacher, most recently an adjunct professor in behavioral science at Palm Beach State College, Florida. He is a graduate of both Winona State University, MN and Florida International University, Miami. Michael is also a retired entertainer [singer/actor], performing primarily as a Frank Sinatra tribute artist under the name 'Michael Matone'. A parishioner of St. Therese de Lisieux Catholic Church in Wellington, FL, Michael serves as a lector and Knights of Columbus member. He is a professional member of the Society of Catholic Social Scientists. The Baglino family, wife and children, live in South Florida. Comments and inquiries are accepted at **dr.mbaglino@gmail.com**

Dr. Baglino is the author of a trilogy of books 'You Only Live Thrice' and 'More from a Florida Catholic' and 'Europe Meets Florida'. Presented is a series of articles and vignettes on religion, psychology, politics and culture. He shows us that God is with us in our daily lives through all our trials, travels and decisions. Insights are garnered from classical education along with our participation in this post-modernist world. Throughout we see splashes of Catholic thought from St. Ignatius of Loyola to St. Thomas Aquinas to a more contemporary and soon to be Saint Fr. Walter Ciszek. Definitely not without humor, Michael presents a down to earth and Catholic perspective to so many of our contemporary issues.

www.ingramcontent.com/pod-product-compliance
Lightning Source LLC
LaVergne TN
LVHW051037070526
838201LV00010B/238